The CHAP

THE BEST OF

Edited by Gustav Temple and Vic Darkwood

B🌿XTREE

Dear Marcus

Happy 30th Birthday!
We brought this book would go
brilliantly in your new bathroom - if
you know what I mean! May it give
you many laughs and even a few things
to aspire to! Lots of Love
Jess and Stu
xx

Put that in your pipe and smoke it

B⬢XTREE

First published 2005 by Boxtree
an imprint of Pan Macmillan Ltd
Pan Macmillan, 20 New Wharf Road, London N1 9RR
Basingstoke and Oxford
Associated companies throughout the world
www.panmacmillan.com

ISBN 0 7522 2590 1

9 8 7 6 5 4 3 2 1

A CIP catalogue record for this book is available from
the British Library.

Designed by M2
Printed and bound in Great Britain by Mackays of Chatham plc,
Chatham, Kent

ACKNOWLEDGEMENTS

Gustav Temple and Vic Darkwood would like to extend the hand of gratitude to the following splendid coves, who very kindly allowed their work to appear in this tome. Mr. Stephen Holden, Mr. Alistair Carr, Mr. Jon Fortgang, Mr. Robert Higham, Mr. Robert Cross, Mr. Medlar Lucan and Brigadier Gordon Volanté. Every effort was made to contact the authors of articles not written by any of the above. We are also indebted to the many readers who have corresponded with *The Chap* over the years, and the fellows who have kept Mr. Saxby on his toes with their Sartorial Agony queries. We are exceedingly grateful to Miss Martindale and Messrs Foulkes, Fry, Gatiss, Madeley, Meades, Okin, Phillips and Tudor Pole for responding to our questionnaires. Finally, we would like to retrospectively thank the contribution made by all those men who, unbeknown to them at the time, donned the most ludicrous knitwear to serve a cause that would one day come to be known as *The Chap*.

The
Ten Commandments
of the
Chap

I
Thou shalt observe the holiness of the hour of high tea and of the cocktail hour

II
Thou shalt not clad thy feet in footwear that is unavailable in the brogue style

III
Thou shalt endeavour to be courteous to all people,
especially those that are lost in discourteousness

IV
Thou shalt eschew the raiment of the sports field when not upon the sports field
(preferably when upon it also)

V
Thou shalt not covet thy neighbour's trilby; rather,
thou shalt offer thine own trilby to the unsuitably attired

VI
Thou shalt share the contents of thy snuffbox with she or he
who displays a mighty hunger of the nose

VII
Thou shalt never fasten the lowest button on thy waistcoat;
if thou art a lady, thou shalt fasten all the buttons on thy gloves

VIII
Thou shalt put cordiality before haste; and eccentricity before punctuality

IX
Thou shalt honour thine accounts with thy tailor and thy bookmaker (eventually)

X
Thou shalt not venerate any graven images
(unless they be of Cary Grant or Grace Kelly)

2000

2001

2002

CONTENTS

2000

Still only
£1.50

ISSUE 3

the CHAP

the CHAP

SPIRITUAL

DRES
FOR

L'AMOUR DE LA MORT

**TROUSER
SEMAPHORE**

plendid Fellow
NETLEY LU

BEHOLD THE COUT

WE ARE THE LA

1
CHAPTER

GRAND TOURISM.

GRAND TOURISM. Preparing for a recent trip to the Americas, we consulted that port-ridden old soak Colonel Fyfe McFilibert-Browne, who gathers dust in the twilight of his condor-winged Queen Anne chair in the MCC. There follows a summary of what, in his opinion, constitute the Dos and Don'ts of the items to include while preparing one's portmanteau.

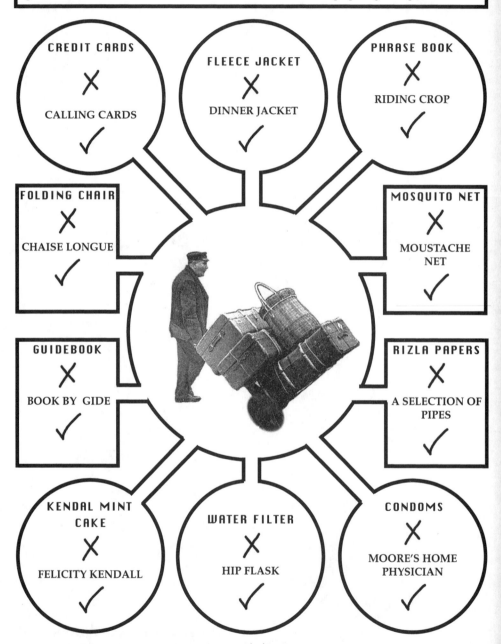

CREDIT CARDS ✗
CALLING CARDS ✓

FLEECE JACKET ✗
DINNER JACKET ✓

PHRASE BOOK ✗
RIDING CROP ✓

FOLDING CHAIR ✗
CHAISE LONGUE ✓

MOSQUITO NET ✗
MOUSTACHE NET ✓

GUIDEBOOK ✗
BOOK BY GIDE ✓

RIZLA PAPERS ✗
A SELECTION OF PIPES ✓

KENDAL MINT CAKE ✗
FELICITY KENDALL ✓

WATER FILTER ✗
HIP FLASK ✓

CONDOMS ✗
MOORE'S HOME PHYSICIAN ✓

MALAISE

Sister Millicent Fond tends to the afflictions of the soul which can befall the modern gentleman.

1. YOUTH

The man being helped by his friends has clearly been afflicted with a rather nasty dose of Youth, a disease which can strike at any age, though the middle-aged are particularly vulnerable. This fellow has drunk too freely from the goblet of Adonis, thus rendering him incapable of clear diction and depriving him of the ability to purchase sensible footwear. The best treatment is for the patient to seek membership of a reputable gentlemen's club, there to indulge in large quantities of port, cognac and cigars. This, coupled with voracious reading of the *Times*, will speed him gracefully into a more dignified age.

2. SPORT

This man has fallen foul of the ravages of Sport. He was found upon a playing field, clad only in breeches, a short-sleeved undershirt and studded boots, clumsily attempting to navigate a leather ball around the field, to the jocular cries of similarly-afflicted comrades. The cure is Baudelaire, of course, or any other poet whose depraved lifestyle resulted in an artistic disease such as TB or syphilis. The sickly stanzas, accompanied by gentle guitar music, will remind the patient that a great poetic mind is best nurtured in the invalid's bedchamber, not upon the playing field.

3. HEALTH

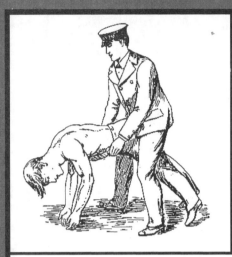

There is a common delusion that vitamins and a high-fibre diet can lead to a spiritually enriched life of the mind. The victim of Health has overdosed on products peddled by so-called 'nutritionists', whose sole aim is to get the young hooked on their highly addictive products, thus enslaving them for life to the commode. The patient will first need his stomach drained in the manner illustrated, then be fed with large doses of expensive chocolates, eggs and pancakes, and any other foods that will stem the flow of bodily waste. The aim of the treatment should be total constipation.

4. COMMUNITY

The ravages of Community can result in total helplessness, and a dependence on one's friends and neighbours for support in every daily action, such as early morning rising, in this case. The patient has lost all sense of identity, regarding himself solely as a cog in

the grand machine of suburbia. Total abnegation of responsibility has resulted in a 'co-dependent' state, where only by including the whole community in his daily rituals can the patient achieve any sense of his own value. The cure is to spread malicious rumours about the town concerning his nocturnal activities in the park; he will soon learn to keep himself to himself.

5. TRAVEL BUG

The first signs to look out for in this increasingly common ailment are matted hair, the inability to wash, and a large multicoloured protrusion on the back. Victims are apt to disappear for several months at a time, usually to the Orient or South America. They will return with various trinkets, baubles and absurd ethnic headwear, and suffer a form of verbal diarrhoea which renders them incapable of speaking about anything except their travels. The cure is to take them on a tour of the literary taverns of their town's bohemian quarter, pausing to quote from fine English writers such as Johnson, or

Dickens: "It is a most miserable thing to feel ashamed of home." (*Great Expectations*)

6. FASHION

This is a highly perfidious ailment currently wreaking havoc on the young. The things to look out for are: (1) Tuning the radio to any other station than Radio 3 or Radio 4 (this is usually followed by frequent visits to record stores); (2) an alarming predilection for expensive urban sportswear; (3) the ability to blend inconspicuously with the common herd, with almost total loss of the superego. There is still no complete cure for Fashion, but various palliative treatments can stimulate the patient into a self-healing process. The most important of these is the acquisition of an unusual haircut, which will help to single the patient out from the crowd, and thus reclaim his right to individual expression.

7. CONTENTMENT

The outward signs of this chronic disease begin when the patient ceases to integrate with the real world, choosing instead to gorge on nest-building pursuits such as DIY, gardening and child-rearing. A dullness in the visage, often leading to 'dead-eye', is the first serious symptom. This is usually followed by an alarming expansion of the girth, and a total rejection of sartorial decency, resulting in the wearing of fleecy tracksuits in public places. At this stage the patient should be taken to Paris, and left there with a maximum of 100 francs. They will soon adapt to the realities of life, and hopefully gain an interest in art and poetry, coupled with a healthy weight loss.

By Angur Masonick

1. IN WHICH NAKEDNESS IS DISCUSSED AND THE CLUBHOUSE REMEMBERED, FONDLY. A FIRST PRINCIPLE IS PROPOSED.

It is a widely held, if infrequently expressed belief, that many people beneath their clothes are utterly naked. Pedants may seek to impress upon a heeding chap the literalness of this opinion. They may have a point. But terrific though an actual bare, naked body certainly is, it is the source of more than just fun. It represents a first principle in the philosophy of grooming, and a fundamental too quickly passed over by impetuous chaps keen to cut to the cloth.

Listen! Because a smelly, dirty or soiled chap is not a Chap at all. The man who is not kempt, or nice, or lovely, the man who appears in public with stubble all over his face like a pustulous rash: that man is a Bloke, and although he may be rich (through football playing or sales) in his self he is poor and ordinary and when he comes close his breath is hot and vinegary, a crisp-fat eructation behind shapeless lips.

So, as we were saying. A clean, supple, stripped body (fabulous breast thrust shamelessly upwards, head dipped in mute delight) forms the basis upon

which every other element of grooming relies. Let us stop for a moment and think about naked people.

Good. There was a reason why we had to do that. Frequently, in his youth, your correspondent was to be found in the company of large, great, hugely grown men. This was in the clubhouse of course, where hours were spent considering those bones of contention which may occasionally arise between even very close friends. And what did your correspondent carry away from the unreserved conviviality of those after-sport sessions? This: that although a Chap may be born low, may in many respects remain low, his lowliness may come to be regarded as incidental. For it is in the body where lies the essence of a Chap's Chappishness, and while clothes may conceal (as well as temporarily postpone) a multitude of sins, a well groomed, maintained and otherwise tidy body speaks more powerfully of manliness than a whole wardrobe of black silk shirts doused in the delicate aroma of Pagan Man. Do you see?

2. A BATH IS TAKEN. EQUILIBRIUM IS CONSIDERED.

Rancid emanations wafting upwards from the body's dankest regions are nasty in almost every way. A shower upon rising and a bath before retiring will keep the skin free from frightening eruptions and also provide one with an opportunity to consider the coming or passing day. One may use oils or lovely, bubbly foam, or one may not.

But consider: the essence of grooming is to enhance, not eradicate the essence of one's self. Equilibrium must be maintained. There are those, and there's no reason why you shouldn't be one of them, for whom the body's pith is as enjoyable as its fruit. Maybe you just like those damp, tangy aromas which hang around after massive exertion. Maybe you just like that sort of thing. You would not, I assert, be alone. But the groomed man realises that there is a time and a place for enjoyments of this sort, and as far as the world at large is concerned he says this: stay clean.

3. THE GAINING AND MAINTENANCE OF SWEET BREATH

Having left our bath and made use of a warm, starched towel we are in a position to get well and properly groomed. Working outwards from the body's interior we meet our teeth. (It is a widely

accepted fact that the mouth carries more and nastier germs than the anus, which is something to think about perhaps, but not right now. Suffice to say, common sense suggests a Chap keep separate brushes for the policing of these two eloquent but sensitive areas.)

And it is not so much the arrangement of teeth which concerns us here (a crooked dentition suggests depth of character and a certain nobleness) as colouring and smell. What, for example, if your mouth has been a little bit neglected and your smile causes others to stand transfixed and horror-stricken as if they'd just witnessed an appalling six-lane motorway smash? Remind them that the Mona Lisa, behind that famously enigmatic smile, was as toothless as a baby, and add that the ill-repair of teeth has long been associated with riotous decadence and the life of the mind.

4. PARTING, SLICKING, PUSHING AND FLOPPING: THE STRANGE PSYCHOLOGY OF HAIR

The semiotics of hair have already been discussed within these pages. So let us now consider the psychology of these unusually elongated, half-mad, half-dead cells, and how they may be persuaded to do as a man wills.

Consider: there is no pain when hair is cut. One cannot exercise one's volition and make it move. Even after death it continues to grow. It may easily be transferred from one part of the body to another, and swells in size and shape according to God knows what principles. It has no purpose. These are clear pointers to the fact that hair is not actually part of the body at all, but an infection not yet recognised as such. And more: that furious chorus of tiny voices prompting you to bellow savage profanities just when you think you might be in with a chance of getting your rocks off? Those are the voices of your hairs, urging you to join them in their crazy carnival of the undead.

Chemists sell mousses, gels, sprays and other mystical embrocations which may go some way to calming hectic hair, but essentially it's a parasite sucking blood and sense from out of your brain and I was glad when all mine fell out.

5. THE SHAVE

OK. This is the big one. Shaving is the final act of the greater part of the grooming ritual and it

should be conducted in a calm, sedate manner, hands free from trembles and other sudden spasmodic movements.

Under a bright, fluorescent light, the mind free from distraction, unsheathe your blade. Wet it and warm it in water. Consider its ruthlessly sharp edge and the damage it may inflict. Feel its weight in your hands. Meditate upon all the futile gestures and meaningless acts of humankind which have brought you, randomly, to this point: naked, alone, unloved. Offer a prayer to your deity although you know your deity is dead. OK. Let's shave.

Once the bristles have gone away and your face is smooth and cool as a marble slab, you'll feel pretty good and everything will be alright again.

Afterwards dab your face dry with a warm flannel and apply a little lotion. Ladies love strong, wild, musky smells. Smells which make them think you're like an unbridled horse. So let your aftershave be both subtle and emphatic, let it speak but not shout, let it sting but not scold and let it let everyone know you're like a fusion of hydrogen atoms in the sack. To live! To die! To shave!

6. NAILS, NASAL HAIR AND EAR WAX: ADVANCED GROOMING FOR EXPERTS

These parts of the self are often skated, as it were, over. Maybe it seems impossible that anyone should be so interested in you that they notice your nails. Most probably you're right to think that. Still.

Grime-encrusted nails may be weeded clean with sticks or doused in a solution of lemon juice, vinegar and salt. But although this will temporarily increase the politeness of your digits, really they ought never to become dirty and in fact a Chap should rarely remove his gloves.

Nasal hair and other unwelcome additions to your olfactory equipment should be dealt with swiftly but privately. Pluck and pick away at the extra matter with tweezers. Similarly do not let ear wax get its foot in your door, obscuring sound and upsetting your sense of balance. It emerges, warm and damp from unused cavities within the brain, and if left in the ear may eventually coagulate into a brittle deformity like a weird and meaningless sculpture. It should be checked for daily and removed by cotton buds like the filth it actually is.

Finally, let grooming become a habit like all your other habits, for this is one area of life where compulsion is rewarded with respect.

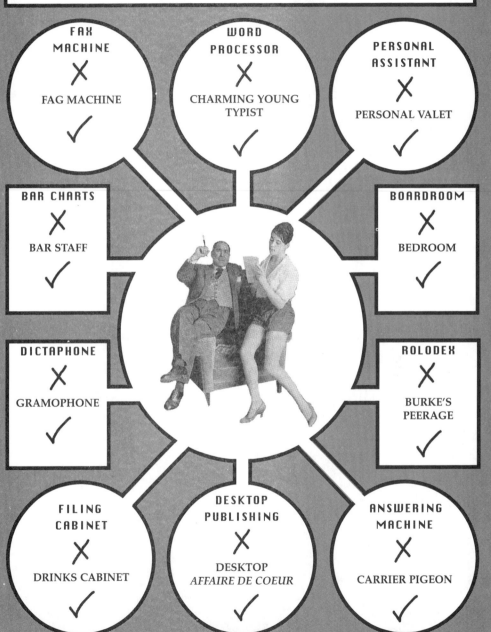

FAX MACHINE
✗
FAG MACHINE
✓

WORD PROCESSOR
✗
CHARMING YOUNG TYPIST
✓

PERSONAL ASSISTANT
✗
PERSONAL VALET
✓

BAR CHARTS
✗
BAR STAFF
✓

BOARDROOM
✗
BEDROOM
✓

DICTAPHONE
✗
GRAMOPHONE
✓

ROLODEX
✗
BURKE'S PEERAGE
✓

FILING CABINET
✗
DRINKS CABINET
✓

DESKTOP PUBLISHING
✗
DESKTOP *AFFAIRE DE COEUR*
✓

ANSWERING MACHINE
✗
CARRIER PIGEON
✓

THE BEST OF 18 THE CHAP

The street kids of American and European inner-cities are said to **"hang tough"** in order to fend off the constant threat of violence in a hostile environment. Here, **DRAKE LOVELACE and MORRIS VEL-VETTE** advocate an alternative technique for the man-about-town who wishes to defend himself, without a consequent diminishing of gentlemanly *savoir-faire* or sartorial elegance.

HANGIN' TOFF

Ah, the filthy business of human competitiveness and human greed lies all around us as we go about our daily business, and nowhere more so than in our decaying inner cities. The humiliation and brutalisation that we receive from our bosses and colleagues are bad enough, but the gauntlet of physical dangers that lie in wait for a man of sensitivity and style as he wafts through the grim urban landscape is often hard to endure.

Street ruffians, not renowned for their keen interest in physics and logic, seem to work on strictly Newtonian principles. That is, the more one takes action to persuade them that they don't want to give you a good kicking, the more they come up with an equal and opposite reaction why they should.

"Oi, you lookin' at my bird?" *"Er, n-no."* "So you don't fancy my girl then?" *"I should say not."* "You sayin' my bird's ugly then?" *"No, not at all. She seems very charming."* "You takin' the piss?" *"No, quite definitely not."* "You think you're something special, don't you? But I can see into your very soul, mate. And what I see is ugly. I ought to smash your face in." *"How does all my cash and a cheque for fifty pounds sound?"* "That'll do nicely, guv."

As you can see, under some circumstances a financial transaction is the only method of calming the savage breast. But for those of us too bound up in the world of beauty to earn a decent living, this is not a realistic possibility. It seems that when it comes to deterring bullyboy tactics the endangered

> ## "Faced with impending fisticuffs the first instinct of a man of sensitivity is to run, run like the wind."

pasty-faced fop is in urgent need of a new system of self-defence. Being well dressed and mild of manner, there will be times when the rougher element, for sheer devilment, territorial reasons or for monetary gain, will approach you with the express intention of doing you bodily harm. It goes without saying that by far the best technique for dealing with such an eventuality is to gather one's trouser cloth up around the knees (to avoid unnecessary bagging) and run like merry hell. But such sanguine opportunities do not always present themselves and there are times when you will be required to think fast and act decisively. As in the unhappy eventuality of being importuned in an alleyway, lift, stairwell, public lavatory or other confined space.

An imminent attack upon your person is not always easy to see coming. A seemingly innocuous situation may rapidly escalate into a full onslaught in a matter of seconds. So keep your wits about you at all times.

One can tell much about a man's temperament and intentions from what he wears and his general body language. You should keep a keen eye out for people wearing sports clothing, trainers, flat caps and mufflers or facial tattoos depicting knives, scissors, tears, spiders or testicles. These are sure signs that the person in question is harbouring criminal intent and eye contact should be avoided under all circumstances. Similarly with body language. A person who stands up and sits down repeatedly on public transport without good reason

Fig. 1

Fig. 2

Fig. 3

or those who stand, sit, stagger, slouch, loiter, whistle, hum or giggle under lamposts in the early hours of the morning are best given a wide birth.

In the following sections, we give a number of techniques designed initially to confuse an adversary, secondly to repel and thirdly to take the offensive.

> Various tactics for repelling attack include: Fig.1 Poking with a cane or knobbly stick. Fig.2 Severely creasing his suit and insulting his tailor. Fig.3 An unusual citizen's arrest technique. Take note that a villain is often identifiable by the wearing of a flat cap and muffler.

Diversionary Tactics

As we have pointed out, and this can't be emphasised strongly enough, faced with impending fisticuffs the first instinct of a man of sensitivity is to run, run like the wind. This instinct should be yielded to immediately. Let us have no truck with petty heroics here. Assuming that, due to being cornered, afflicted with athlete's foot, generally lacking in fitness or merely disinclined to indulge in physical exercise, you are unable to extricate yourself from danger sufficiently swiftly, then you should read on.

Much like a bird of prey, a common street thief does not respond to rational thought. A low animal cunning coupled with a lust for physical satiation account for all of his mental activities. He is genetically programmed to respond to bright lights, sudden movements and the sight of blood.

Ironically it is these very instincts which make him vulnerable to a well-thought-out set of diversionary ruses.

Ensure that you never leave the house without a pocketful of brightly coloured beads or marbles. In the event of attack, these should be thrown pell-mell in a direction opposite to that in which you want to escape. The average mugger will be thrown into momentary confusion, and will either stand dumbstruck or chase after these glinting objects, giving you adequate time to flee. Similarly, a watch or cufflink may be utilised to harness sunlight and reflect it into the eyes of a potential assailant, burning his retina and slowing down his killer responses.

If this sudden movement theory proves ineffectual then the opposite tack can be tried. Total immobility is not with out its attendant risks, but when in extremis, it may be your best option. Orchestrating a realistic fainting fit will have the probable effect of a total loss of interest on the part of your attacker but there is always the outside possibility that finding you wholly recumbent he may see you as a more attractive target for a good kicking. A psychopath will generally show no mercy. It is advisable to judge carefully your foe's particular state of mental health before attempting a lie-down.

Repelling Attack

Once you have established a mutual understanding with a bullyboy that he firmly intends to break every bone in your body and is disinclined to be deterred from his cherished course, then it is time to progress to means of repelling his attack.

When he lunges at you with his huge potato hands and great slavering jaws, it is important that you show no fear. Your first effort should be directed at keeping him at a comfortable distance. To these ends a cane, rolled umbrella or knobbly stick should be used in the manner shown in Fig.1. This is only likely to slow down his advance but gives you invaluable moments to consider your next move. Try shouting a deterrent such as "Push off, you great ruffian!" or "You'll regret this some day!" and hope that it makes him see sense.

Once he lays his mits on your three-piece worsted, the show is on and the gloves must come off. No one should be allowed to toy with your immaculate attire and get away with it. Before he is able to lay one on you, try dragging his jacket off his shoulders and down around his elbows Fig. 2 and at the same time taunt him mercilessly about the inadequacy of his tailor and the inferiority of his cloth. The chances are that his increased fury will only make his entanglement worse.

Finally, if you find yourself being attacked from the rear, it is well within the rules of engagement to grab your adversary's ankles as illustrated in Fig.3. In this position he may be carried harmlessly to your local police station where he can be dealt with by the proper authorities.

Taking the Offensive

There comes a point at which even a man of pure reason is made to see red. Enough is enough. "Get off my case daddio, I ain't takin' no shit, no more," as the saying goes. The worm turns and all hell is let loose. It is at this point in the midst of an unprovoked assault that a fellow has to take up weapons and change defence to offence.

UNDERSTANDING THAT STREET PHRASEOLOGY

In times of extremis it is frightfully important to know your enemy. Memorising the following glossary will equip you well for survival on the street.

Pants – *Your tailor leaves much to be desired.*
Magic – *Wizard.*
Wickid – *Devilishly good.*
Yo, bitch – *How d'you do, madam?*
Larging it – *Having a grand old time.*
You dissin' me? – *Run, run like the wind.*
Boys in the hood – *Neighbourhood watch.*
Caning it – *A spanking good time.*
Respect – *Protocol.*
A big up – *Charmed, I'm sure.*
Homeboy – *Weren't we at the same school together?*
Sorted – *Composed.*
Kickin' – *A bit of a knees up.*
Roll another phat one – *Spin another platter.*
Bro's before ho's – *I have recently become a member of the MCC.*
Mashed – *A bit chipper.*
Chill – *Fancy a glass of Chablis?*

The carrying of knives, knuckledusters, firearms and the like is simply not on. But you might be surprised how many of the everyday items that a chap carries about upon his person can be swiftly converted into offensive weapons if need be.

Take for example the humble sock suspender which can be converted in a trice into a makeshift catapult or a sturdy garrotte. Or a common-or-garden tortoiseshell comb which when dragged aggressively along the underside of an attacker's nose is as excruciating as anything invented by the Inquisition.

But how demeaning it is to have to dwell on such unpleasantness. In the final analysis only one thing will keep you safe on our urban thoroughfares, and that is respect. Take a leaf out of George Melly's memoirs. When confronted by a gang of teddy boys down a dark alley one evening, his only reaction was to stare manfully ahead and recite a few verses of Dada poetry as if it were the most natural thing in the world.

Try it some time. Who would mess with you then? Respect due, George.

Angur Masonick *examines the delicate matter of locating, courting and pleasing the ladies.*

1. THE MATTER IS CIRCLED, TENDERLY.

It is a truth universally acknowledged that any man in possession of good trousers and firm teeth must seek a lady with whom to share these things. For although we live in very progressive times indeed, many of the finer – and also cruder – aspects of wooing remain as mysterious to a chap as the intricacies of his own digestive system. Younger chaps may find parts of this matter hard to talk about. Others may find them hard to do. That's natural. There have been times when your own correspondent has found it hard, and there have been times when he has not. That's just how it tends to be with the ladies.

But this is not a matter we should approach fearfully. Ladies will not scratch or bite or eat us. That sort of thing exists only in the febrile mind of the adolescent. Ladies should instead be regarded as embodying so much that a chap might wish to claim as his own: kindness, gentleness, finely-

TOWARDS...
A
PHILOSOPHY
OF
WOOING

shaped hair. And yet perhaps you still feel some fear. Perhaps you have yet to be experienced by a lady. Maybe you have on occasion enjoyed and been enjoyed by a lady, but were left with a terrible sense of emptiness, as if you had considered every inch of the world through a highly powered microscope and yet were unable to discern any trace of yourself within it. Well that's just too bad. Sparking up chicks is a hell of a job, so let's just get down to it.

2. AN ENTIRELY HYPOTHETICAL, IMAGINED AND MADE-UP SITUATION IS SUMMONED, AND WITHIN THAT FICTIONAL CONTEXT AN ADVANCE IS MADE.

Let's just say, and this isn't beyond the bounds of credibility, that you know, or know of, a lady. Perhaps you've encountered one at your place of work. Perhaps her name's Veronica, and maybe she sits at the desk in front of you, and you're as familiar with the way her hair sweeps the nape of her perfect neck as you are with the palm of your own greasy, calloused hand. Perhaps you find it hard to talk to her, and that your carefully prepared bons mots dribble wetly out of your mouth, down your chin and on to your shirt, so that she shrinks from your bizarre presence like a lovely little rabbit bolting down a hole. What exactly are you doing wrong here, and how may it be rectified?

3. TWO PROBLEMS.

1. Firstly, you appear to Veronica to be an unnatural and crazy freak. This she finds off-putting. You've done well by deciding in advance exactly what it is you'd like to say to her, but when you speak it sounds like there's a little animal - a vole perhaps - stuck in your throat. Veronica likes all animals, including voles, and in fact at the moment she likes them much more than she likes you.
2. There is a vacuum where your confidence should be. You are like a droopy old vegetable at the bottom of the fridge that not even a student would eat. Veronica must be persuaded that you embody, in a very fascinating way, all the attributes of a gentleman. Your correspondent must be allowed to intervene.

4. YOUR CORRESPONDENT INTERVENES.

"How goes it, Veronica?" I would purr, fixing her with my fully operational eyes. "I gotta tell you babes, you're looking hot hot hot. What say you to a little drinky after work? There's a cosy Pitcher & Piano around the corner. We could be alone."

5. GAUGING THE MOOD, TONE AND VEIN OF A DATE. EARLY PROBLEMS NIPPED IN THE BUD.

Happily installed in a booth, a gin and tonic in hand, you are in a position to begin wooing Veronica in the old-fashioned way. Look her in the eye. Listen to what she says. Probably you won't understand a lot of it, but nod appreciatively anyway. Keep nodding. Let the conversation develop at its own pace. Interject, interpolate, inveigh if it seems at all appropriate, but bear in mind that this is not the place for expostulation. If you do expostulate prematurely, a polite cough behind your hankie may go some way towards clearing the matter up.

6. THE END OF THE EVENING. THE EXERCISE OF RESTRAINT. A SMALL COMPLICATION.

Veronica is so sweet and lovely that the evening's conclusion approaches like a terrible punishment or even death. Never mind. The purpose of this first encounter has been merely to break the ice, to straddle the gate, to establish a foothold from which we may undertake a more serious ascent of Veronica's fabulously steep slopes. Take your leave gallantly. Part with a chaste peck on the cheek. No matter how she begs, pleas and implores, let the evening end there. She may demand you to satisfy her, again and again, all night long, but resist. See her home, bid her goodnight, and return to your compact bachelor pad, where I will be calmly waiting for a frank account of the evening's proceedings, in the full and certain knowledge that Veronica only went out with you in order to get closer to me.

7. WE APPROACH THAT MOMENT IN WHICH MAN AND WOMAN ARE UNITED IN EPIC, SPEECHLESS BLISS.

Let us suppose now that Veronica, for whatever perverse reason, continues in this foolish tryst (God knows why – there was nothing obscene about those poems, it wasn't me who stole her shoes, and I don't understand why they've moved my desk to the other side of the office). Together, you return from a delicious meal at your local pizza outlet, your faces greasy with the sheen which food from that particular establishment tends to produce.

"I say, Veronica," you venture. "What about a chipped mug of tepid Nescafé at my place? We could listen to my new Mogwai CD. Or if you don't like Mogwai, perhaps The Suede. We could fool around." Veronica finds herself enormously unmoved. You have not captured her interest at all. Your correspondent must again be allowed to intervene.

"Veronica," I would say. "I am a man, with all which that implies. You, I suggest, are a woman, subject also to certain basic needs." Here I would pause for effect. "Let's get naked and urgent and let's do it now!"

Pushing open the front door we fall carelessly upon each other. She tears at my very expensive clothes. We move from the sofa to the sink to the scullery to the utility room to the library and reach a breathless conclusion in the lavatory.

"God!" sighs Veronica. I am forced to agree.

Now do you see? Your approach was meandering. Mine was direct. Yours was vague. Mine was clear. Yours was feeble. Mine was audacious. These are the watchwords when wooing a lady. Veronica won't be forgetting your correspondent in a hurry.

ADDENDUM

So it is in these ways that a chap should conduct his affairs with the ladies. He should concentrate on one at a time. He should seek to be there when they need him. He should respect their dimensions and listen to their words, and he should not seek to make a move on Veronica, right? Just tread carefully there, mate, that's all I'm saying.

LETTERS

SIR,

Do any of your readers find it difficult to obtain a decent Pousse Café? The last time I had one of these delicious Cocktails was from 'Robert' in the American Bar at the Casino Municipal, Nice.

Recently, after an excellent luncheon at the Burger King in Slough, I ordered a 'Golden Slipper'. I was disappointed to be informed that this was not available as they were fresh out of Eau de Vie de Dantzig, which as you know is Dantziger Goldwasser.

Bad show all round, don't you think?

DAVID LE NOBLET OF PRESTON,
LONG CREDON, AYLESBURY, BUCKS

SIR,

I count it as a great personal triumph that the ghastly continental practice of drinking black coffee in my workplace has recently been supplanted by taking tea, indeed, obscure leaf teas, made properly in a teapot. Moreover there is talk of procuring a silver cake stand in the not-too-far-distant future. It is these tiny raindrops that will turn the tide and open the floodgates. I cannot sufficiently express how gratifying was the realisation that I am not alone.

C.M.G. RYAN, CASSIOBURY, WATFORD, HERTS

SIR,

Recently I witnessed a mischief-maker of the lower classes pelt a wood pigeon with an apple. How is the gentleman to act when faced with acts of such depravity?

P.J. MARTIN, PALMERS GREEN, NORTH LONDON

SIR,

In days gone by I seem to remember that in gentlemen's conveniences there used to be notices by the egress saying "Please remember to adjust your dress before leaving". Surely, in these days of an ageing population whose memories may not be so sprightly as they once were, these useful reminders should be reintroduced. They would undoubtedly prevent much social embarrassment and nights spent in the cells of Streatham, and other, police stations.

MAJOR BETRAM BURBERRY-MACINTOSH,
LONDON SW16

SIR,

I recently purchased a copy of *The Chap* from my local branch of Borders in Brighton and was appalled to find that someone had inserted a note inside. Obviously some devious tick had taken it upon himself to 'spike' your marvellous mag with an itchy little display of underhand sabotage.

Written, in cheap ballpoint as one could find in the lesser respected turf accountant, was the word 'W**KERS' and on the reverse; 'PILLOCK'. I was shocked and dismayed and my only solace was in the fact that I had discovered it before someone of a lesser stomach had.

Anyhow, I removed the note and placed it between the pages of a well-known amateur photographers' publication, feeling that there it may be better appreciated.

DUX VESPASIAN BELLORUM

2001

The **CHAP**

CADDING
ABOUT

HAT
DOFFING

PIP

DIVINITY LIES IN...

The **CHAP**

ISSUE 5

JOHN
WAT

THE TRUTH
ABOUT
SMOKING

CON
COS

The **CHAP**

ISSUE 6 £1.50

£1.50

LESLIE
PHILLIPS

UNDERSTANDING
THE LADIES

DECADENT
DIEPPE

DRESSING FOR WRESTLING

LET US JUDGE A MAN'S SOUL BY THE CREASE IN HIS TROUSER

2

CHAPTER

HANDSOME

Vladimir Shokov embarks on a crusade against vulgarity, making some new friends in the process.

An acquaintance of mine recently found himself in need of a public convenience, having just refreshed himself with several light ales in a West End tavern. He had the misfortune to be within the vicinity of Piccadilly Circus, the only conveniences being those situated in the bowels of the underground station. Upon entering the gentlemen's unit, my acquaintance received something of a shock. The entrance of the lavatories was carpeted with various pools of human effluence of a particularly nasty odour; a vagabond appeared to be performing a cursory grooming ritual at the filthy enamel sink, and, worst of all, a young fellow seemed to be pleasuring himself at one of the urinals.

Now, my acquaintance is rather a sophisticated sort: he never leaves his rooms without an exquisite suit of clothes, a pair of gloves and an ebony cane. It fairly brought tears to my eyes when I pictured his elegant figure forlornly micturating at one of the urinals, amid this scene of frankly Rabelaisian dimensions. To call it Sodom and Gomorrah would be to bestow it with far more glamour than it deserves. It was, in short, a scene of the most abject vulgarity.

When this experience was described to me, I could only nod my head in mute recognition of all-too-many similarly depraved sights which I had witnessed within this city. I realised that vulgarity, as opposed to the more popular evils such as biological warfare, genetically-tampered foodstuffs and Johnny Foreigner's noxious cheeses, is by far the greatest threat to the future of humankind.

Perambulating through the chilly thoroughfares of this city, my home and my nemesis, I began to observe the scale with which vulgarity had crept into the lives of the townsfolk. A young fellow, clothed in a rather unattractively cut suit with an outrageous four-button jacket, was dashing along Shaftesbury Avenue. He had clearly missed a luncheon appointment, perhaps due to becoming engrossed in one of the city's fine 17th-century church façades; in his hands he was clutching a tin-foil container, from which he was spooning into his mouth some revolting oriental concoction, while maintaining an ignoble canter along the pavement. I immediately felt pity for the poor fellow, having myself missed many a luncheon appointment due to architectural appreciation, so I offered him help.

"Discard your perambulatory snack, sir," I said to him, "and join me for a light repast in a pleasant eatery."

His reply cannot be repeated here, but suffice it to say it contained a rather unnecessary series of profanities. I shook my head in dismay as I watched him merge with the passing throng, hardly pausing to toss his spent foil container into the gutter.

I had little opportunity to reflect upon this display of vulgarity before being confronted by another example. As I turned into Great Windmill Street, a young lady stepped into my path, wearing pancake make-up, fishnet stockings and a single piece of red patent leather obscuring her modesty from the world. Without so much as a by-your-leave, she invited me to avail myself of her body, adding that her residence was in the vicinity. Now, my libido is as powerful as the next man's, but I must confess a certain fondness for the subtleties of formality and subterfuge which normally precede a visit to the courts of Venus.

Needless to say, my second offer of luncheon was flatly refused.

I decided on a rare solitary lunch, and proceeded in search of a modestly priced though refined eatery. I found myself upon The Oxford Street, which I believed to be the home of such establishments. However, the friendly little restaurants offering simple home-cooked meals that one could wash down with a glass of ale were nowhere to be seen. In their stead were a succession of establishments whose function I found it difficult to determine. Loud music emanated from within the cavernous interiors, where flashing lights illuminated scores of youths, many of whom sported a curious type of headset with a black stick

pointed at their mouths. It was the middle of the afternoon, yet these youths disported themselves in a manner one associated with evening revelry. That is to say, they shouted, jostled one another for attention, gyrated their hips to the thumping music, and loitered around the cubicles at the back of the establishment. All in all, it was a scene of the most obscene vulgarity. I hastened to escape, only to find a succession of similar emporia lining the street.

Curious as to whether I had been mistaken in my geographical calculations, I ventured into another of these establishments to enquire. I approached a spiky-haired youth wearing a headset, and asked whether any charming little eateries still existed on The Oxford Street. The question seemed to confuse him, and he responded with something of a non sequitur: "What size are you, mate?"

Reflecting upon this for a moment, I surmised that it was an indecent proposal of a thoroughly depraved nature. I left the place without comment.

Droplets of rain had begun to fall; much of

including one which shot out of my shirt-sleeve on a species of metal pulley.

Finally, the day arrived when I knew I was ready. Armed with my collection of cigarette lighters, a slim volume of Symbolist verse and some 67 bons mots, I set out for the West End of London.

You must understand that I was in something of a frenzied state of mind. Perhaps I was not quite in full control of my faculties, but my purpose was clear: I felt that I had been selected by the gods of elegance and sophistication to begin the crusade against vulgarity. My subsequent actions, I believed, would clean up the city once and for all, paving the way for the practitioners of virtue, beauty and refinement.

My first stop was Chinatown, where I located the establishment most popular with the yuppies (Oh yes, I now knew what they were called, for I had studied their habits in the newspapers). Discreetly placing myself to one side of the take-away counter, I waited for my 'friend' to appear.

Sure enough, up he trotted, or rather sprinted, in search of his tin-foil container of comfort food. He was just about to fling his credit card at the diminutive oriental behind the counter and bark out his order, when I gently touched him on the sleeve. "I think it is time for lunch," I said with a smile, opening my jacket just enough for him to see the cut-throat razor nestling there.

"I see," was his brief reply. He clearly understood, and swiftly pocketed his credit card. We walked side by side to Great Windmill Street, where it took a short time to locate the address of the harlot (Yes, I now knew her moniker, too). We ascended the two flights of stairs, and I knocked on the door. At this point, the yuppie tried to make a dash for it, but I halted him by whipping out my volume of verse and reading him a stanza of Verlaine. This held him rooted to the spot until the door opened. "Well, hello!" said the harlot, "do come in." She tried to show us some sort of price list, but I counteracted with a few witty bons mots, before thrusting her my card and inviting her to lunch.

The three of us strolled up to The Oxford Street, where, with some difficulty, I managed to locate the particular emporium of depravity which I had previously entered. I found the be-headsetted urchin I had spoken to (whom I now knew to be a vendor of poorly-made, over-priced factory clothing). "My good man," I said

the crowd surged into the glittering emporia to seek shelter. I, for my part, remained alone on the pavement, a light drizzle moistening my brow. A half-remembered line from a forgotten film suddenly came to mind: "One day a real rain will come and wash all the scum off the streets..."

---- ∞ ----

Over the next six months, I immersed myself in a rigid training schedule. Surrounded by the 'vagueness with precision' of Fauré's sonatas for violin and piano, I concocted intricate blends of India and China teas, and spent sleepless nights sampling them, perfecting my cup and saucer control. I mastered new and complex knots for my enormous collection of ties; I starched my shirt collars till they nearly cut my cheeks. My personal grooming routine would last for hours, until I had perfected dazzling acrobatics with a cut-throat razor. I studied cigarette lighting techniques, until I was able to successfully light four cigarettes in a few seconds, with various lighters concealed about my person, to him, "I believe it is time for your lunch break!"

He clearly had some difficulty in understanding me above the infernal din in the shop. I shouted directly into his plastic mouthpiece, using a cheap ruse to lure him out of the shop: "My size isn't in stock," I shouted. "You'll have to go to the other branch." He flung off his headset and dumbly followed the three of us out of the shop. Of course, I had already decided where we would go for lunch. I planned to leave nothing to chance on this day of reckoning. I led the dumbfounded trio to 'Laurelei', a delightful little eatery in the heart of Soho, happily untouched by the creeping tentacles of vulgarity.

I let them order whatever they wanted, not that there was much choice (an integral part of the rehabilitation process, for I have noticed that too much choice in consumer-related commodities leads inevitably to vulgarity). I managed to engage the three misfits in a fairly successful trialogue during the meal. Yuppie found that Harlot and himself had attended the same school, and Youth had apparently sold Yuppie a pair of trainers once.

When the meal was over, I demonstrated my skills in the tea-making milieu, having previously arranged this with the proprietor of Laurelei. The trio were visibly impressed. Harlot asked some intelligent questions, such as whether the variable annual rainfall in Ceylon affected the flavour of the teas. We got on to the subject of personal grooming, and Youth brought up the tricky sub-genus of personal hygiene. Harlot was able to enlighten him on one or two scores, and then Yuppie launched into an eloquent tirade against expensive safety razors, resulting in a round of applause from all of us.

It was during coffee and liqueurs that the ice really began to melt. Harlot got out her B&H Superkings (by now, she had graduated to the more acceptable 'Monica'); Yuppie (Philip) whipped out a rather splendid Havana cigar, and Youth (Gary) surprised us with a willingness to smoke at all, drawing out a packet of Marlboro Lights from his tracksuit trousers. Ah, how we smoked! How we laughed! My collection of lighters proved useful, particularly during a tricky moment when all four of us put a tobacco product to our lips at the same time. Philip was the recipient of my

swing-motion double-action Zippo, deftly executed at the flick of a wrist.

We adjourned to the Fox and Hounds, next door to the Laurelei, for a few rounds of cognac. By then, I knew that my work had been done. With a few simple lessons in civilised living, I had shown a trio of dormant souls that we did not need vulgarity to foul up an otherwise beautiful existence. It was our divine right to simply say No Thank You to vulgarity and Yes Please to refinement.

---- ∞ ----

I still bump into Philip occasionally on Shaftesbury Avenue, as he leisurely ambles back from a three-hour lunch at the Laurelei, and we pause to exchange a few lines of Verlaine in front of a splendid Georgian portico.

Monica is now the manager of a delightful little patisserie in Soho, where I often drop by for a cup of tea and some petits fours.

The last time I saw Gary, he was cocking a snook at a brigand of sportswear-clad ruffians on The Oxford Street. They were wearing Nike; he was wearing a Hawkes worsted three-piece and sporting a magnificent cane. The foppish delivery of Gary's acerbic witticisms soon had the better of the ruffians, whose bovine attempts at one-upmanship merely sucked them deeper and deeper into their quagmire of vulgarity.

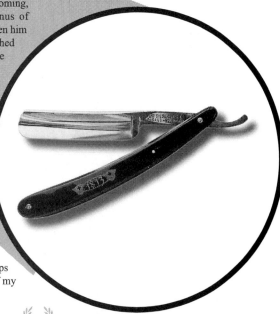

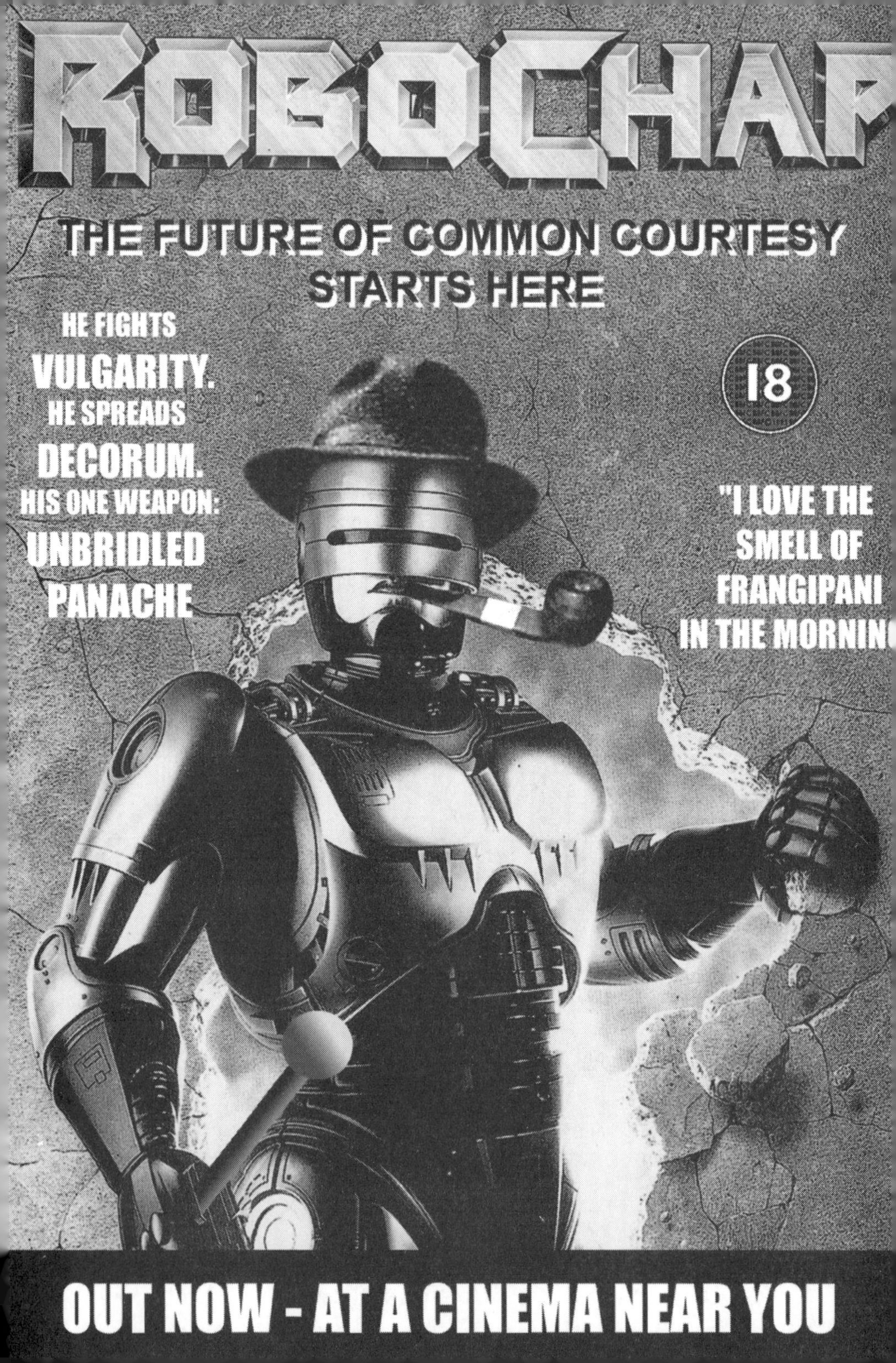
ROBOCHAP
THE FUTURE OF COMMON COURTESY
STARTS HERE
HE FIGHTS
VULGARITY.
HE SPREADS
DECORUM.
HIS ONE WEAPON:
UNBRIDLED
PANACHE
18
"I LOVE THE
SMELL OF
FRANGIPANI
IN THE MORNIN
OUT NOW - AT A CINEMA NEAR YOU

DESIGNS FOR LIVING. We consulted the fashionably reclusive Baron Longchaise du Bidette, who rarely leaves the opulent sanctity of his grade-1 listed mansion on the edge of Regents Park, on some hints towards creating a living space condusive to the most beautiful reveries. Here are the Baron's Dos and Don'ts of interior design

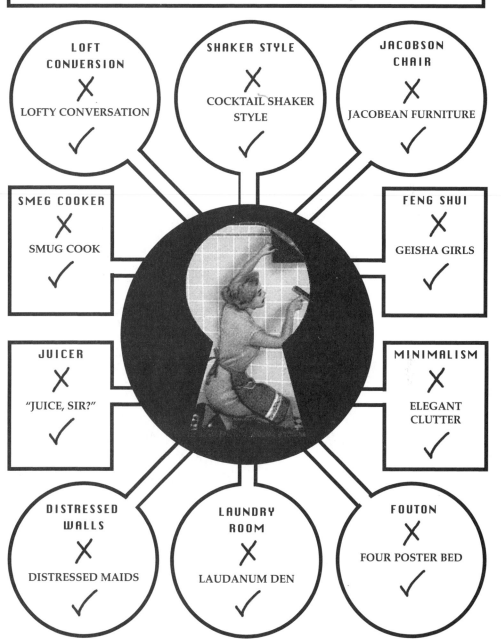

LOFT CONVERSION
X
LOFTY CONVERSATION
✓

SHAKER STYLE
X
COCKTAIL SHAKER STYLE
✓

JACOBSON CHAIR
X
JACOBEAN FURNITURE
✓

SMEG COOKER
X
SMUG COOK
✓

FENG SHUI
X
GEISHA GIRLS
✓

JUICER
X
"JUICE, SIR?"
✓

MINIMALISM
X
ELEGANT CLUTTER
✓

DISTRESSED WALLS
X
DISTRESSED MAIDS
✓

LAUNDRY ROOM
X
LAUDANUM DEN
✓

FOUTON
X
FOUR POSTER BED
✓

Saint George ELASTICATED ARM BANDS

Sick and tired of dunking your newly starched cuffs in your mulligatawny soup? Fed up with never being able to see your hands? Want to avoid debilitating conditions such as 'Monkey Cuff' and 'Ape Sleeve'? Other than purchasing a shirt that actually fits or spending vast amounts of money on corrective surgery, you only have one realistic course of action, and that is to invest in a pair of Saint George Elasticated Arm Bands. Fun to wear and manufactured from 100% shiny-effect metal, these stunning requisites are exactly what you need to get you noticed in all professions that involve extensive arm usage. And what's more, the ladies love 'em.

"Lummy guv'nor, give that fellow a big hand."

St. George Elasticated Arm Bands
Available from:
**Hall Bros.,
7 Rowlands Road,
Worthing, West Sussex.**

SIR,
In recent visits to public houses I have noted numerous examples of persons forced, it seems, to drink their beers directly from the bottle. Surely in these supposedly "never had it so good" times, the licensed victuallers of Britain can do something about this apparent shortage of glasses?

MAJOR BERTRAM BURBERRY-MACINTOSH
LONDON SW16

SIR,
While on a recent tour of the battlefields of Flanders and Picardy, I was delighted to observe that Belgian boy scouts still wear shorts, and corduroy ones at that. Well done, the Chief Scout of Belgium whose name, alas, escapes me for the moment.

MAJOR BERTRAM BURBERRY-MACINTOSH
LONDON SW16

SIR,
One finds it damnably difficult to purchase a decent gasper over here, not a Dunhill or a Sobranie Cocktail in sight. These foreign johnnies wouldn't know a proper ciggie if it exploded in their sombreros. Some damn fine Cuban cigars can be had for slightly less than the price of an hour with a street girl but, as even that is beyond my meagre means, I have to make do with cigarillos Americanos. Vulgar concoctions of roasted weed but entirely necessary if one needs one's nicotine appendage. A chap without a cigarette is hardly much of a chap at all really.

CPTN IAN GILMER (DSO & BAR RTD)
PANAMA

SIR,
I have for some time been considering the acquisition of a monocle, being shortsighted in one eye as the result of a mis-spent youth. The problem is that after many an hour in front of the looking-glass, I am confident that such an eye-piece would satisfy all æsthetic demands in my right eye, though it is in fact my left eye which requires the ocular amendment. Have you any suggestions that might resolve my pernicious predicament?

HATHERSEDGE TWEMLOW, CANNING-STREET,
LIVERPOOL 8, LANCASHIRE

SIR,
Why not a double-page souvenir of Gregory Peck? It's time we girls got our fourpence worth.

MISS M.A. STAGIN, LESLIE, FIFE.

SIR,
I recently entered a branch of a respected book merchant to purchase myself a book, for the purposes of engaging my faculties during the long hours spent waiting for my local omnibus.

Imagine my surprise and horror when the assistant offered me a book which she described as a "paperback", principally, it would seem, due to the inferior nature of the cover. Whilst prepared to accept the book for purchase (I planned to negotiate a reduced fee for removing this second from their stocks), I had to alter my plan when I realised, upon closer inspection, that *the pages of the folio had already been cut.*

THOMAS F.W. RIBBITS, WANSTEAD, LONDON

GLOBAL CHAPITALISM

The Chap is profoundly stirred by reports of gentlemanly activity in far flung parts of the globe. It seems that, thanks to our sterling efforts within these pages, pockets of savoir-faire and panache have begun to spring up in remote cities. The first of these reports concerns the gentlemen of Yemen.

GENTLE YEMEN
Situated on the coast of the Red Sea, opposite Ethiopia and below Saudi Arabia, Yemen has never been a place associated with fashion like Milan or Paris. But it seems that a subtle transformation is taking place among the menfolk of the capital Sana'a. They have taken to wearing tweed jackets over their traditional cotton robes, known as *thopes*. Tweeds such as herringbone, Harris and Prince of Wales are the most popular, usually colour co-ordinated with the thope, which comes in white or shades of brown or green. The accessories include a tooled leather belt embroidered with gold thread, and a traditional dagger, or *jambiya*, in a turquoise sheath. The look is rounded off with a racy cotton headscarf known as a *kefir*. *The Chap* can only bow to such exotic foppery of the highest order, and is hoping to buck the trend for such fashions here in Britain.

BOLIVIAN BOWLER
There are over one hundred different styles of hat in Bolivia, where hats are worn not just as a fashion statement or as protection against the sun, but because the head is considered the most sacred part of the body. One of the most distinctive hat styles is that worn by the Aymara women in the capital, La Paz. They wear a grey or brown type of bowler which locally goes by the quaint name of a *bombin*. While the vast majority today are made of felt, some are still made from rabbit hair, as they all were originally. The origins of this fine 'titfer' are shrouded in mystery. One theory is that an enterprising merchant, having mistakenly imported a huge quantity of men's bowlers, tried to pass them off as ladies' hats. If this is true, it proved a very lucrative move, for in the 1930s the Italian firm of Borsalino began to mass-produce the bowler hat for export to Bolivia. Today, no self-respecting peasant lady would be seen without her bombin.

A SINGULAR FELLOW
In an altogether less remote part of the globe, the Negresco Hotel on the Promenade des Anglais in Nice, was recently host to a remarkable confidence trickster. He claimed to be Prince Ismael of Sandakan, arriving in a chauffeur-driven Jaguar to take three deluxe suites. A regular flow of attractive female visitors, champagne dinners and diamonds from Nice's prestigious shops all helped to run up a bill of £260,000. The charming impostor turned out to be Ismael Nabou, a Mauritian of no fixed abode. He was so convincing in his role as a jet-setting royal playboy, and so generous with his tips, that the hotel staff did not once question his credentials. When the police turned up one morning and arrested him, the staff were almost sorry to see him go. The Chap doffs his homburg to Mr Nabou, wherever he may be now.

THE CHAP QUESTIONNAIRE
LESLIE PHILLIPS

The subject of our questionnaire in this issue is one of the few remaining fellows worthy of being called a Chap. In the '60s he was the epitome of charm and savoir-faire, cutting an impeccably-groomed dash as he breezed his way through the quintessential English films of the era. His casual air of bespoke sophistication would have looked out of place in anything other than an open-top sports car, and he was always ready with a witty bon mot for any passing young lady. Leslie Phillips is now 76; he still pursues the noble craft of the thespian with skill and dedication, and he maintains his hirsute responsibilities with dignity and panache.

1 In what type of clothing do you feel at your most seductive and alluring to the ladies?

Something terribly loose.

2 What items of clothing do you consider the greatest offences against sartorial decency?

The short-sleeved shirt.

3 Do you have any strong views on the fashions followed by today's youth?

No - anything goes.

4 Is there any occasion during which you might consider wearing training shoes?

No, they damage one's insteps.

5 Do you still sport a pencil moustache?

Yes, if you can spot it.

6 If so, does it require a lot of maintenance?

No - light work.

7 Do you believe there is a place for any kind of beard in today's society?

Yes, for the right part. It saves the use of spirit gum - horrid.

8 Are you a user of either a mobile phone or a personal stereo?

Only in extreme emergencies.

9 Would you like to see a ban put on either of these?

Only if overused.

10 Can you help us answer this age-old conundrum: where the devil can a fellow get a decent dry Martini?

I'm not into booze.

11 You have always been known as something of a hit with the ladies. Any tips on dealing with today's feminists?

Let them make the moves.

WITH ONE BOUND

HE WAS FREE !

Angur Masonick seeks sanctuary from his own oppressive perfection.

EXTREME FUN ENJOYED DANGEROUSLY AND AT THE EDGE

I feel, and am considered, and am, very, very attractive. I am, in almost every respect, quite pointlessly blessed. I am rich. I am clever. I am hauntingly beautiful. The walls around my bed bear the fingerprints of more filthy women than I am able to recall. The cupboard in my cookerless kitchen – I never dine in – contains only capers, cocktail gherkins and vodka. My flat is in a block in a neighbourhood in an area where angels fear to tread lest they be corrupted by the shocking, squalid enjoyments hourly enacted hereabouts, by the equally blessed and fantastically dressed decadents with whom I fraternise and sororise. You come to die where I live because life after living here would be a living death. No sooner has an impulse wandered drunkenly into the private members' club of my conscious mind than it is acted upon, guiltlessly and without legal repercussion. For reasons we need not go into here, I've barely done a stroke of paid work in the last three years and, it is my weary duty to inform you, the fun I have is more extreme in nature than people even such as yourselves are capable of imagining.

AND YET . . .

And yet on waking most evenings in my crowded king-size bed, sated and aching, skin gnawed to rawness by a coterie of gruesomely insatiable Europeans, I find I am compelled immediately to leave my enormous domain because I am filled with fear, and boredom, and I am bored of fear and afraid of boredom. For lately it occurs to me that I have pursued pleasure so vigorously, and for so long, that at some point and without noticing I have overtaken it, and am now stalked by its bitter, vindictive spirit which wants my soul - God knows why, it's a disgusting thing, soiled and infectious - even though I am hauntingly beautiful, frequently decline payment for my commercially viable poetry, occasionally direct pop videos, erect sculptures, commit only those crimes suggested by fashionable magazines and have the unusual gift of knowing in advance what sort of weather to expect.

Consequently, I am now drinking in the old fashioned way – i.e. efficiently and alone – in an area I rarely visit. Outside is my automobile, a mechanism so phallic that when at rest I am forced to cover it with a specially commissioned prophylactic, lest the minds of the poor and disadvantaged grow pregnant with desire. And even with things being as they are – me, alone but beautiful (hauntingly so, or did I already mention that?), clever, rich, meteorologically precogniscent etc., I find I am filled with an immense, drenching sense of tedium, as if each empty, pointless moment might last for years, only to be replaced, eventually

and unnoticeably, by another vast, empty moment which itself stretches thinly towards infinity, each monster-sized monument to monotony passing ever more slowly, until no more moments remain. Apparently I often think like this. And so, chief among the many valuable, unique and brilliant thoughts currently surging through my powerful brain, is this one: my life is a living heaven from which I am compelled to flee although I have no idea why, where to, or what for. And this thought having been thought it is with only the mildest surprise that I awake the following morning in a Singapore hotel, slightly chesty, a precociously hung Vietnamese fondling the well-packed haversack I tend to keep in my car.

MEANS OF ESCAPE No. 1: TRAVEL. SADNESS AND DISILLUSION IN THE EARTHLY PARADISE OF A FAR EASTERN BEACH COMMUNITY OF WESTERN GRADUATES VOCALLY ESPOUSING ANARCHO-LIBERTARIAN PRINCIPLES, MANY OF WHOM ARE WRITING DYSTOPIAN, POST-HIPPIE-LORD-OF-THE-FLIES-TYPE NOVELS.

It is evening. The sun hangs level above the sea, its final brightness caught occasionally in the folds of distant waves. Beside me is a girl. We are strangely united despite the lack of a common tongue, our mute but mutually delightful congress having proved a more

direct path to truth and beauty than religion, philosophy or art. We savour for a while the purity of this moment, which exists neither in time nor space, but which somehow contains the enormity of both. Not only have we escaped our lives, we have escaped life, with all its tedious tribulations and admonitions.

"Tripsbrewblackmazzieswhizzdieselsmack." A kid, a wizened golem, tugs at my ankle.

"No."

"Tickets to DJ Migraine-toothpaste-walkman batteries-Spice Girls Jigsaw-last week's Observer, Travel Card Zones 1–4." He's more useful than the Internet.

"No thanks."

"Whatcha want? I get it. Easy."

A pause. Heavenly Cipher next to me stirs, wakes, takes my hand in hers, moans, returns to sleep. "Nothing." Golem eyes me quizzically. He looks about a hundred years old.

"Thanks. I don't want anything."

"What you doing here then?"

"I came for the waters."

A further pause during which Golem visibly ages by another seventy years. He squints, draws a circle in the sand with the tip of his flip-flop then gobs artfully into its centre. "Water's full of shit," he says.

"I know. I was misinformed."

MEANS OF ESCAPE No. 2: A SPIRITUAL JOURNEY. A GRAIN OF SAND IN THE WORLD

And so I am alone again in my cavernous domicile, my many self-induced illnesses exacerbated by the carcinogenic orb that hovers perpetually over the city, and also by the sun. I have not escaped. I begin to think about God, and Buddha, and Gaia and Blake and Yeats and Crowley. And so it is with only the mildest surprise that I awake next morning on a bed of uncushioned wooden slats, bound only in sweat-soaked swaddling, a tender young monk fondling the well-packed haversack I tend to keep in the car. Several weeks of silent, intentionally futile manual labour pass – I dunno, it's a Zen thing. I ply the speechless spiritualists with questions and each day ends with them beating me to bloody pulp. It's all most enlightening. Finally I am brought before the Master.

"You seek an escape from the spirit-crushing tedium of life, from the compulsion to pursue distant goals which, having been attained, prove as tedious and unsatisfying as the state of affairs from which you flee?"

"That's about the size of it."

"You find your body punishes your mind, which likewise castigates the body?"

"I don't actually mind a certain amount of punishment but..."

"My child. Consider the grain of sand upon the beach."

My heart sinks. "Yeah yeah. I know. When the doors of perception are cleansed man will see things as they really are, the world in a grain of sand." Bastard.

"No my child. You are as a grain of sand in the world, and the world is as an atom in the particle that is the universe. You are less significant than..." He drifts off in silent reverie. Several hours pass. We speak not. I am frozen in terror, reheated by panic and then made tepid by a terrible torpor: let it not be that I, Angur Masonick – rich, clever, beautiful (hauntingly so, many have said) and also of course, weather-wise – am less significant than a microbe of dust drifting gently but pointlessly through the eternal night of unexplored space.

Finally the Master speaks: "I say, Jenkins, wouldn't it be wizard to go scrumping again. Have you learnt your verbs? Mummy'll be home soon. Nanny says to ask the Farmer first but I don't think we should. Jenkins, would you like to see my toad?"

Weeping gently, your correspondent leaves. *I cannot go on. I go on.*

DECADENT DIEPPE

Cyprian Ferneaux has the extraordinary ability to travel through time, making him a highly sought-after correspondent. He takes us on a walking tour of Dieppe, at various stages in its history as home to exiled members of the English Decadent movement.

Readers, join me on my quantum trajectory and let us glide towards Dieppe in the year of our Lord 1895. The writers and artists of the English decadent movement have been driven to this charming little town on the north coast of France, exiled by a resurgent philistinism at home. Events came to a head with the recent arrest of Oscar Wilde at the Cadogan Hotel. The popular press reported that Oscar was carrying a copy of the Yellow Book as he was led away by the police. Soon an angry mob gathered outside the offices of the Bodley Head, demanding the removal of Beardsley as the Yellow Book's art editor. The mealy-mouthed British public has come to equate Beardsley and his art with Wilde's so-called crimes and the general decline in morals. The irony of the whole debacle is that the book in Oscar's hand was merely a popular French novel called *Aphrodite* by Pierre Louys, which happened to be bound in yellow. Nevertheless, six hundred gentlemen felt threatened enough to decamp to France that evening on the night boat, when only sixty would normally do so.

Dieppe is bordered to the east by the church of Notre Dame de Bon Secours, and to the west by a chateau rising out of a grassy hill. We can also see Dieppe's

peppermint-bricked casino, upon whose elegant terrace poets, painters and assorted dilettanti congregate on summer evenings to drink vermouth and enjoy the company of intelligent and unattached ladies. The exquisite music of Saint-Saëns emanates from the glass-domed concert hall. English lords in the habit of losing their fortunes in the baccarat rooms can be seen walking out and shooting themselves among the beds of begonias.

Suitably attired in a light linen suit, boater and buttonhole, we set out with the firm intention of paying a call on Aubrey Beardsley, now established at the Hotel Sandwich. We leisurely stroll along the promenade, from where we can see the celebrated cocotte Cleo de Merode shamelessly disporting herself on the beach, surrounded by panting admirers. We pass on, choosing instead to admire the ornamental flowerbeds laid out before the hotels. Scarlet salvias, lobelias and waxy begonias all clamour for our attention with their subtle fragrances.

We notice an ashen-faced young man with drooping eyelids and a clipped moustache, analysing and dissecting the scene before

LEONARD SMITHERS AND SOME RATHER LOUCHE FRIENDS ENJOYING THE FINE WINES OF DIEPPE

him. It is none other than the author Marcel Proust. We introduce ourselves, and beg that he share with us his reveries.

"Alas, is it not possible, my dear Monsieur Ferneaux, to discern in the freshest flower those just perceptible signs which to the instructed mind indicate already what will be the desiccation or fructification of the flesh that is today in bloom, the ultimate form, immutable and predestinate, of the autumnal seed. Is it not so, do you not think?"

But we must confess to only seeing the flowers in their prime, and beyond the flowerbeds, the sun blazing over a glittering sea, with little blue-painted, russet-sailed fishing boats upon it. We bid Proust adieu, and move at a brisk pace through the narrow streets around the Tour St Jaques. Here we encounter Walter Sickert and his cohort of cockney impressionists from the New English Art Club, almost blocking our way with their easels and stools. The luminous quality of the light attracts them and makes them reluctant to leave. Stepping gingerly over the cobbles, we finally find ourselves at Beardsley's door.

A strange spectral figure greets us, delicate and consumptive. 'A face like a silver hatchet with grass-green hair' – Wilde's description of the tragically talented illustrator comes to mind. He wanly smiles and beckons us into the room. The blinds are drawn against the harsh light of day. Beardsley has no use for daylight, luminous or otherwise, and claims only to work by candlelight.

He also tells us he is unable to draw anywhere but London, and is now working on his prose masterpiece, *Under the Hill*. Perhaps so, but beneath the elaborate garb of one of his Helens or Isoldes, the seasoned eye can detect the unmistakable form of a soignée Dieppe bathing girl.

Rejected in his own land, the rest of the world now comes to cultivate this extraordinary genius. Today, Beardsley's visitor is a Russian of easy-going cheerfulness with a curious mask-like face; he is introduced to us as Serge Diaghilev. He tells us that Beardsley's art is causing something of a revolution in Russia. The talk is of producing designs for Pushkin's *Eugene Onegin*, which he has been reading in a French translation.

We now adjourn to an alfresco gathering around the tables at the Café des Tribuneaux, where the irretrievably louche Leonard Smithers has gathered a circle of decadent writers and artists around him. The talk is animated and boisterous, as the recent events in England are discussed. Smithers proposes to found a new publication to rival the Yellow Book, which it has been said turned grey overnight with Beardsley's removal. A cheer goes up when he announces that Aubrey will be the editor, and Arthur Symons the literary editor. It will be called *The Savoy*. A word here about Leonard Smithers: from his bookshop on the Strand he has amassed a fortune publishing scholarly editions of oriental erotica and deluxe editions of Latin authors. Wilde has said of Smithers that he always brings his books out in editions of three: one for the author, one for himself, and one for the police. It was rumoured that he also had in his possession a book bound in human skin.

As more wine is called for, we notice Ernest Dowson sitting alone, in a state of melancholy slumber, a glass of absinthe before him. Gentle, affectionate, drifting Dowson, desolate and sick of an incurable passion. He has lived a life of romantic isolation, haunting the Les Halles quarter of Paris and the London docks, drawn to the condition of the poor and dispossessed. Dowson is never without the company of a common harlot, and claims they are cheaper than hotels. Yesterday he was involved in a drunken brawl with a local baker, and brought before the magistrate. A deputation arrived and let it be known that Monsieur Dowson is one of the most illustrious English poets. "Thank you for reminding me," said the magistrate, "I will therefore imprison the baker."

Dowson enquires of the newly-arrived Londoners about the prevailing mood in the English capital. It seems that all is not well. Poets are forsaking their velvet collars for tweed suits, absinthe for pints of ale. The barrel organs are playing a jingoistic tune; the Café Royal is deserted . . .

1897, TWO YEARS LATER

Oscar Wilde's favourite restaurant in Dieppe is the Café Suisse. Here we find him, sporting a Basque beret and looking rather unlike his foppish former self. The most striking reminder of his two years' hard labour is the compulsion to continually rearrange things on the table before him. Oscar explains: "I had to keep everything in my cell in its exact place – and if I neglected this even in the slightest I was punished, and the punishment was so horrible to me that I often started up in my sleep to feel if each thing was where the regulations would have it, and not an inch either to the right or the left. And the terror haunts me still, involuntarily my fingers make order where anything is disarranged."

Among the company at the table is Dowson, who presses upon Oscar the necessity of acquiring a more wholesome taste than that which caused him so much trouble in England. They agree to visit a house of assignation of Dowson's recommendation. The news spreads quickly, and soon a cheering crowd is accompanying them. When they reach their destination, the crowd remains outside. Presently Wilde returns. He announces in a low voice: "It was like cold mutton. But tell it in England, for it will entirely restore my character."

SOME TIME LATER

The Savoy published six issues, for which Beardsley struggled through days of utter languishment and recurrent haemorrhages to produce his most accomplished work, before succumbing to illness at the age of twenty-six. Dowson, not much older, was found in a London guesthouse – starvation and neg-

BATHERS ON DIEPPE BEACH by AUBREY BEARDSLEY

lect were the cause of death. Wilde now lies in Père Lachaise cemetery, having barely breathed his last before his body erupted with fluids from every orifice.

We find ourselves again at the spot where we had our memorable encounter with Proust. The flower-beds are now brown and barren; the sea is grey and sluggish. The hotels stand before us in their winter mode, with the shutters firmly fastened. Proust's words have returned to haunt us, and there is a distinct chill in the air. We recall some lines of Dowson's:

I cried for madder music and for stronger wine
But when the feast is finished and the lamps expire
Then falls the shadow, Cynara, the night is thine
And I am desolate and sick of an old passion

ALTERNATIVE LIVING. We consulted that mystical guru of the gaming table Neville Soupçon D'Agincourt about the alternative lifestyle choices currently finding favour among university drop-outs, shamans and bored housewives in the London Borough of Kensington and Chelsea. Here are Soupçon D'Agincourt's Dos and Don'ts of alternative practices.

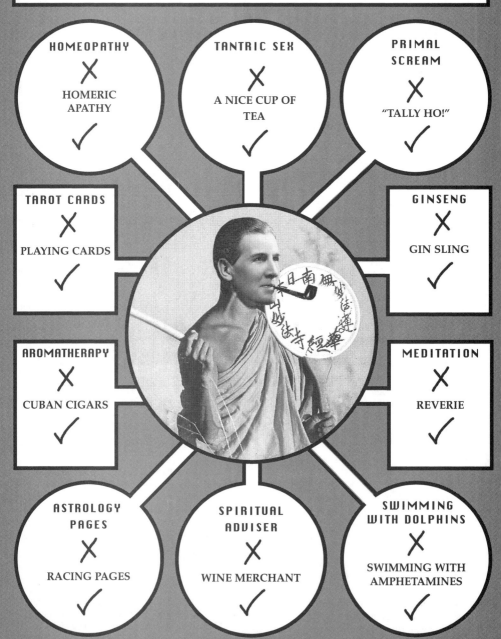

HOMEOPATHY
✗
HOMERIC APATHY
✓

TANTRIC SEX
✗
A NICE CUP OF TEA
✓

PRIMAL SCREAM
✗
"TALLY HO!"
✓

TAROT CARDS
✗
PLAYING CARDS
✓

GINSENG
✗
GIN SLING
✓

AROMATHERAPY
✗
CUBAN CIGARS
✓

MEDITATION
✗
REVERIE
✓

ASTROLOGY PAGES
✗
RACING PAGES
✓

SPIRITUAL ADVISER
✗
WINE MERCHANT
✓

SWIMMING WITH DOLPHINS
✗
SWIMMING WITH AMPHETAMINES
✓

CADDING
ABOUT

Sheridan Coxcombe gives timely advice for the gentleman who wishes to go abroad without the incumbent loss of social grace and sophistication.

THE FOLLIES OF THE YOUNG ARE NEVER TO BE UNDERESTIMATED. Rather than squandering their cash on ephemeral pleasures, shunning work and aggravating the constabulary, which is what the young are for, they nurture irrational fears about ill health and poverty, squirreling their vast salaries into Personal Equity Plans. Judging from Youth's comical efforts with razor, comb and brush, they would have much more to gain from a Personal Grooming Plan. But it is during that magnificent period of the year known as 'the hols' that they really let themselves down. Their principal mistake lies in restricting themselves to two or three weeks' holiday a year. Many of my acquaintances would consider three weeks of *work* quite sufficient to fill up a year, as long as they were spread evenly throughout lengthy periods of chronic inactivity.

Youth's other grave error is in choosing 'adventure holidays'. Of course, travel agents are guilty conspirators in these ugly trends. Their brochures bombard the weary eye with promises that read more like threats: TREKKING IN THE HIMALAYAS! WHITE WATER RAFTING IN VENEZUELA! SNOWBOARDING IN SWITZERLAND! Pardon my naïveté, but surely the whole point of a holiday is to rest? With photographs of grinning Scandinavians leaping up mountains, dressed from head to foot in orange and purple lycra, these brochures will produce in the gentleman nothing more than a powerful urge to collapse on a chaise longue and embark on a laudanum-fuelled journey into the mind.

The other activity that seems to be popular among holidaymakers is that of visiting the 'sights'. First of all, may I point out that the most valuable parts of the world's ancient monuments can be viewed at leisure within the warm, comfortable halls of the British Museum. The bits that were left behind were either too cumbersome to carry or, frankly, not all that interesting to look at. The other problem with tourist sights is that they are rarely located within easy reach of a tube station, like the British Museum. They are usually at the end of strenuous journeys under a relentless and merciless sun. The contemplation of a pyramid, statue or menhir can be thoroughly ruined by the thought of the hazardous, suit-ruining return journey that awaits you, once you have made a cursory inspection of said monument and taken the requisite photograph (which will be of no subsequent interest to anyone, including yourself).

Finally, on the subject of observing natural phenomena, allow me to quote Ian Fleming, who chronicled his own travels in a delightful little tome entitled *Thrilling Cities*. In the section on Honolulu, he is invited to go and view the volcano Kilauea, which has just erupted:

"It makes the Fourth of July seem like a lighted match," said my informant, "you'd better go quick." I said of course I would. I didn't. I was tired of aeroplanes, and this terrestrial blow-off seemed to me an aspect of the private life of the globe into which it would be 'bad joss' to pry.

So, how can a Chap ensure that he chooses a holiday destination where he is likely to enrich his mind, replenish his soul and meet similarly sophisticated people? There follows a brief summary of the aspects of foreign travel that should be carefully considered

That fastidious style guru Hardy Amies gave some highly useful tips on dressing for the holidays in his *ABC of Men's Fashion*:

1. Never wear shorts except actually on the beach. No continental, except a German, will wear shorts even going to the beach. He knows them to be inelegant and often considers them indecent.
2. All short sleeves look ghastly. If you feel hot, then roll up your sleeves but never above the elbow.
3. Sandals are hell, except on the beach where you want to take them off, or on a boat. And worn with socks they are super hell.
4. Wear an expensive belt. See that your wristwatch strap doesn't look sweaty.
5. Unless you are going to a very simple Austrian village, I think it is wise to take a dark suit to wear at night.
6. There is nothing elegant about real ski clothes as a travel outfit; in fact it is a distinctly scruffy idea.

before leaving the comfort of your rooms.

1. Once you have decided upon which country you'd like to visit, always, without exception, go to the capital city. These tend to attract the more civilised, cultured tourist, so you'll be in good company. They are also the only cities where you will find a genuine bohemian quarter, and a substantially sized red-light district.
2. Make sure that there are no activities available with even the remotest suggestion of 'adventure'. Adventure tourism and eco-tourism imply a strong long-hair presence, which can lead to hair-braiding and other immoral activities being performed openly in the streets.
3. Do not go anywhere where the local religion precludes alcohol or pre-nuptial sex, unless, like Casablanca or Cairo, for example, several decades of Euro-tourism have slackened public morals and temporarily blinded policemen's eyes.
4. Try to dispense with the pointless question "What shall we do today?" early in the holiday – in the hands of the wrong hangover, it can lead to dark thoughts on the futility of life in general. The question

is pointless because you will inevitably end up taking an eight-hour stroll around the city, prompted by an initial foray in search of a cup of tea, which, alas, was never to be found. For this reason, choose a very old city: they are far more pleasant to wander about in all day.

5. Avoid museums at all costs, unless they are of genuine interest, such as a museum of pipes, or moustaches. Most museums assume that foreign visitors are deeply interested in seeing some frayed old parchment outlining the city's copper industry regulations in 1743, and such like. It can be very difficult to muster much interest in the history of somewhere you have spent the best part of three days.

6. Thoroughly investigate the local drinking situation – or the drug scene, if booze is off the cards. The advantages of getting drunk in foreign cities are manifold: you meet more people; not speaking the local language loses its importance, as a drunk person always believes he is making perfect sense, whatever nonsense he is spouting; drunken behaviour always generates more exciting anecdotes. Would Ernest Hemingway be such a legend if the tales of his life in Cuba and Spain were about visits to Franciscan churches and browsing round the souvenir shops?

7. Adopt the local dress code as much as possible. If the men all wear silk pyjamas under a cotton dress, go and purchase some immediately. This

will give you an outside chance of not being mugged, at least by a myopic thief. It will also brighten up the days of the beggars and hawkers, perhaps bringing the first smile to their lips for several years.

8. Do not, under any circumstances, get a suntan. They are vulgar, unhealthy and turn a ghastly shade of orange as soon as you set foot on British soil again. Also, it may arouse suspicion at the local employment office, should you be a state-funded personality.

To conclude, it would seem that the only place a Chap could possibly go on holiday is Mexico City. It is a capital city whose air is so polluted that any activity at all is actively discouraged, following the near-death of an English tourist who collapsed while playing tennis; a very loose adherence to Catholic tenets means that alcohol, drugs, prostitution and gambling are to be found on virtually every street corner; Mexico City was founded in 1521 on the site of a previous Aztec capital, so it's bloody old; the locals sport a rather charming pleated shirt of light cotton and smart woven hats; the city has a combined red-light district and bohemian quarter the size of Leicester; and there is an efficient metro service that can ferry you from one alfresco monument to the next, so you can enjoy them on your daily stroll without ruining your clothes or setting foot in a museum.

THE LOST ART OF
DOF

**By our etiquette correspondents
Torquil Arbuthnot and Nathaniel Slipper.**

We live in a world where, sadly, too many gentlemen no longer wear hats. By hats I mean, of course the trilby or the Homburg, the bowler or the Panama, and not the baseball cap worn forwards, backwards or sidewards, nor the Patagonian goat-herd's bonnet (as worn by the embarrassing, yet not embarrassed inhabitants of Camden Town). With the decline in hat wearing has come a concomitant, and regrettable, dwindling in the elegant art of doffing. It is not just a question of lifting one's hat from one's head and then replacing it, as if lifting a saucepan lid to check the devilled kidneys are coming along nicely. That different social situations demand different doffs should be as well known as the etiquette of holding a polite conversation with one's ne'er-do-well brother-in-law.

The standard doff (or the "Watson") is used when encountering those who are perhaps not one's social equals, but nevertheless worthy of a gentleman's acknowledgement, for example the bank manager, the vicar, the local bobby. In this situation grip the crown of the hat lightly in the right hand, lift an inch or so with a forward tilting action, and replace immediately in one smooth motion without breaking your stride. Imagine that the brim of your hat contains a barely manageable amount of milk, and you wish to pour a little into a tea cup, without spilling a drop of it or slopping any over the sides.

If the "doffee" is some distance away, such as the far side of a croquet lawn, then the hat should be lifted completely from the head so that the doffee can see daylight twixt hat and head (the "Chamberlain"). A variation of this doff, (the "delayed Chamberlain") whereby the hat is held aloft for several minutes, is used when standing on the deck of a colonies-bound P&O steamer, bidding adieu to those on the quayside. N.B. When wearing

FING

a soft hat lift by the crown; hard hats (the bowler, the "topper") should be lifted using the brim.

On meeting one's equals or, should such people exist, one's betters, use the Watson doff but lift the hat the merest fraction of an inch. This doff (the "Salisbury") should, of course, be accompanied by a greeting and a comment on the weather, perhaps with an apposite quote from Baudelaire or Mallarmé.

The appropriate greeting to chaperone the doff is of course, "How do you do", said as a statement rather than asked as a question. To one's lessers, one should initiate the greeting. Always allow one's superiors to greet first. The correct answer to "How do you do" is "How do you do", with the slightest of emphasis on the word "you". This is all that is truly necessary, all is well with the world, and one can now continue one's perambulation without continuing the conversation, and not appear even the slightest bit rude.

When meeting ladies on the street, remember that it is incumbent upon the ladies who know you to make the first gesture of acknowledgement, and for ladies unknown to you to proceed with their business as if you were never seen.

Whilst in the bloom of youth, and still a dashing bachelor, should a pulchritudinous young lady pass one in the street, it is just permissible to doff one's hat "gallantly" (the "Logan") (Fig. 1). The right arm should be raised so the upper arm is perpendicular to the pavement, then the hat doffed completely till the lower arm is vertical. The whole arm should then assume an aesthetically pleasing L-shape.

On rare occasions one can utilise the simultaneous doff-and-usher gesture (or the "Shuttleworth-Robinson gambit"). This should be used when taking a blushing debutante to dinner.

One removes the hat completely and segues the doff into a sweeping gesture while simultaneously opening the door (of one's roadster or of the eating establishment) and ushering the young lady therein. However, there is, it must be said, something raffish about this doff, and it should, perhaps, be restricted to those males who affect suede shoes and have a penchant for loud waistcoats.

One is never too young to start doffing. Schoolboys should not raise their caps or boaters: the "Harry Wharton tug" (Fig.2) is the correct way of doffing the cap or boater. With right forefinger and thumb, simply tweak the peak or brim downward a half-inch or so. There is no need to resettle the headgear to its original position as a young stripling's hair's natural springiness will, providing the youth is not too enamoured of brilliantine, accomplish this unaided.

Distressingly, one will encounter in public certain persons one does not wish to encounter; persons who, for reasons best known to themselves, H.M. Constabulary have not yet put in "chokey". Good manners prescribe one should acknowledge them rather than affect not to see them or make a vulgar and pagan gesture. In such a situation the briefest of schoolboy tugs on the brim, accompanied by one's best military stare and a curt inclination of the head (known as the "Pierrepoint"), is the correct response. Do not, however, flick the brim of your hat with your forefinger while favouring the ruffian with a narrow-eyed glare: one is not Mr John Wayne encountering Mr Lee Marvin in the high street of Dodge City, and one may find oneself in the unflattering position of chasing one's hat down the street in the manner of the droll Mr Chaplin.

Finally, on no account accompany the doff with any kind of bow, be it a Prussian neck-click (der "von Leese") or a Mediterranean doubling-over (il "ferissione"). This sort of behaviour is not seemly in an Englishman, but is the province of, respectively, the unfeeling Nordic type and the excitable Latin.

Suggestions for further reading:

Gerard de Nerval: *Reflexions sur l'Enlevements des Chapeaux*
Anon: *Tailor & Cutter Vol. 23*, Spring 1942 'Correct Deportment of Military Headgear'
Robert Burton: *Anatomy of Doffing*; an analysis of what Doffing is, its kinds, causes, symptoms, prognostics, and several instances of it; Philosophically, Medicinally, and Historically.
George Du Maurier: *Trilby*

Fig. 1. **The Logan** - Note the aesthetically pleasing L-shape formed by the right arm.

Fig 2. **The Harry Wharton tug** - The correct mode of doffing for stripling youth.

THE CHAP QUESTIONNAIRE
Mark Gatiss

Earlier this year, *The Chap* was highly excited at the prospect of watching *The League of Gentlemen* on the television. He settled himself comfortably on the chaise longue, arranging his Persian cat Mou-mou in the folds of his dressing gown, while little Ahmed switched on the set. Imagine our surprise when, instead of the familiar opening credits of the classic black-and-white film starring a dashing Jack Hawkins, a contemporary programme with a somewhat more risqué content appeared on the screen. We instantly became huge fans of *The League of Gentlemen*, and invited one of the trio, Mark Gatiss, to put some answers to our questionnaire.

1 What is your idea of complete sophistication?

Watching *The Wicked Lady* with a team of Czech gymnasts at my beck and call.

2 Who would you describe as the quintessential English gentleman?

Who else? James Mason.

3 Where do you think the best-dressed people are?

Kensal Green cemetery.

4 What items in your own wardrobe are you particularly attached to?

a) Sword stick; b) Pearl-handled Beretta; c) Waistcoat with discreet skull motif.

5 What single situation has been the greatest challenge to your wardrobe and your personal grooming skills?

An unscheduled visit by Princess Michael of Kent to a Limehouse opium den where I was spending Mother's Day.

6 What work of art would you like to own?

Caravaggio's 'The Supper at Emmaus'.

7 What book or poem has been the most inspiring to you?

The Adventures of Sherlock Holmes.

8 Which view from which window would you describe as a 'portal to poetic perfection'?

The view from the Tiepolo Room (or water closet) in my ninth home in the San Vidali, Venice, looking out over the biscuit shop.

9 What quality has been the greatest benefit to your love life?

Evil.

10 What advice would you give to a young man who aspires to being a gentleman?

Good manners cost nothing.

11 What aspects of contemporary life cause you the most annoyance?

The misappropriation of apostrophes.

12 What items of clothing do you consider the height of vulgarity?

The black shoe/white sock combination.

FINGER CLAMPS

The Thoroughly Modern Remedy for Unsightly Work-a-Day Hands

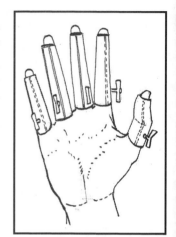
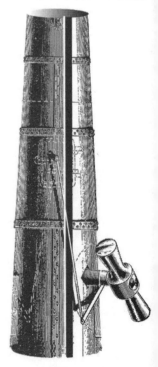
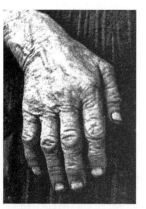
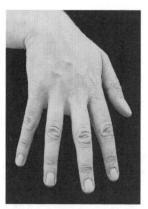

Howard Spent investigates

STRIKING A POSE

Words, words, words – dear reader, where will it all end? Publishers assail us with hundreds of thousands of new titles each year, daily newspapers denude hillsides of forestry to fuel our insatiable appetites, politicians spout interminable rhetoric and the 'chattering classes' continue to do what they do best – chatter. We are drowning beneath a deluge of meaningless verbiage. I beseech you to stop where you are. Rest a while, consider your options and then boldly throw a shape or two.

If actions speak louder than words, then it might be concluded that a particular form of inaction, known as 'striking a pose', provides a subliminal whispering gallery for the human psyche. In the cut and thrust of human interaction, a few seconds of firmly held immobility can speak volumes.

A man of upright character and stoic corsetry may find himself balking at the idea of what at first glance may seem a vain and, let it be said, effeminate occupation. You will no doubt be seized by nightmarish visions of Marcel Marceau and those particularly lame 'living statues' who spray themselves gold from head to foot and loiter pointlessly in city centres around the globe. But these are merely music hall versions of what is in fact a serious science.

Striking a pose properly demands an in-depth knowledge of human psychology, acute eye-to-hand co-ordination and an impeccable sense of timing. Like a tardily delivered bon mot, a pose struck a split second out of place may lose virtually all of its impact.

You will soon find that situations you are accustomed to approaching with a great deal of garrulousness will run far more smoothly when punctuated with a few moments of eloquent freeze-framing.

Take, for example, the jilting of a lover. The process of breaking it off with a lady can be fraught with anxiety. The chances are that your paramour will not take too kindly to being dumped unceremoniously and without coherent justification. She is liable to become heated and unreasonable, and will start asking difficult questions such as: "Did you mean it when you said you loved me?", "Is there somebody else?" and "When are you going to pay back that three grand I lent you?" By striking a pose something akin to Rodin's 'Thinker' and contorting one's face into a mask of harrowed grief and limitless regret, you will be able to gain vital seconds to consider your next move. She will assume that, although you are resigned to it being 'all over', you still feel the loss like a white-hot blade cutting into your heart. You, on the other hand, will be calculating the precise number of sentences required to extricate yourself from this embarrassing predicament and install yourself in the snug bar of the Crown and Anchor.

Similarly, when entering a cocktail party or other social event, striking a pose is a highly effective tool for getting noticed and breaking the ice. Give careful consideration to the exact dash you wish to cut. Will you be serious, intellectual, bohemian or merely approachable? Striking out into the social ether, you will immediately find yourself swarmed upon by like-minded individuals and ladies keen to make your acquaintance.

Over the following pages you will find an appraisal of several commonly used poses, some highly effective and others that are best avoided. With practice and discernment you will develop a repertoire that will hold you in good stead when dealing with the world in general, and will prove an invaluable implement for use socially, in business and for pleasure.

The Subtle

Understatement and a profound love of leaning against classical architecture are qualities to be encouraged in a young man. But on no account incline at an angle of more than 7° from the vertical. The geometry of the Infinite is an unforgiving mistress.

The Mesmeric

It has been proven time after time that ladies are sadly vulnerable to the pantomime self-confidence techniques of quacks, charlatans, double-glazing salesmen and Robbie Williams. Messianic gesturing is the first and last refuge of the scoundrel.

The Self-Conscious

This fellow is so consumed with self-regard that he spends many hours a day trying to hide the podgy imperfections of his midriff. The distending tendencies of gluttony, indolence and hard liquor should be worn with certitude and pride.

The Epicene

The threatening behaviour of ruffians is often hard to repel, but the last thing they will expect you to do is to 'vogue' shamelessly. Brocade, lace and effeminacy can be as frightening to a bullyboy as looking down the barrel of a loaded AK47.

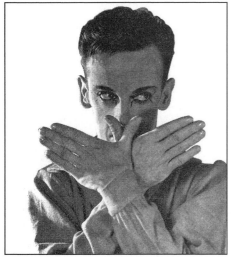

The Theatrical

Profound bashfulness and an unhealthy interest in that degraded art form called 'mime' has lured this man into making a nincompoop of himself in polite company. Imitating the trajectory of a sick bird in flight is no substitute for riveting conversation.

The Wily

It can be greatly advantageous during high-powered business meetings to throw oneself into eccentric contortions in order to wrong-foot one's adversaries. Holding this singular pose for a good ten seconds will give you invaluable time to review your tactics.

The Malodorous

No amount of manly posturing can disguise a chap's insecurity about his personal hygiene. This fellow believes that he has pulled the wool over his ladylove's eyes by fiendishly disguising a surreptitious sniff of his own armpit as rugged machismo. He has not.

The Gigolo

Occupying a corner at cocktail parties, affecting a posture of wistful melancholy and wearing unsettlingly louche attire, this fellow might be regarded by some as a lost soul adrift in a sea of torment. He is, in fact, a practised predator of other men's wives.

The High Street

The 15th Earl of Camardenshire believes that elegance is the only criterion by which one should judge one's fellow man. Of course, he is right, but he does himself no favours by preferring the cheeky élan of Miss Selfridge to the manly domain of Savile Row chic.

The Conscientious

As eloquent as a mention in Burke's Peerage, a rakish hauteur singles this chap out as a man of stock and of principle. A career in advertising has allowed him to bring vital product information to the masses, putting into practice his deeply held socialist beliefs.

The Replete

Whilst attending tea parties at one's Maiden Aunt's, it can be difficult to demur on that final piece of coffee cake without offending her feelings. Feigning communication with an unseen muse will assure her that her baking abilities aren't on the wane.

The Enigmatic

This saucy coxcomb spreads doubt and disharmony by adopting a demeanour of machiavellian intrigue. Such affectation may have worked wonders in the Court of Versailles, but is of precious little use in his present occupation as a newsagent in Chipping Ongar.

CRIMES OF
THE GENTRY

*If a life of drudgery and toil for the corporate beast is not for you,
allow **Torquil Arbuthnot** and **Nathaniel Slipper** to gently guide
you into a far more glamorous and civilised career in crime.*

In order to sample more than three draughts of absinthe a week and
ensure a regular supply of Turkish tobacco, one needs to be able to put
one's hands on ready money, and plenty of it. But how is this to be
gained? Can one retain the respect of one's companions at the
Hellfire Club after a day spent totting up ledgers or selling
second-hand cars? Our motto is, if it involves computers
and fluorescent lighting, then someone else must do it
(although this motto does sound better in Latin). The quintessential chap would normally be a law-abiding sort of fellow,
who looks one straight in the eye and can be left safely alone
with one's sister or collection of T'ang dynasty snuffboxes.
However, after a few reverie-inducing puffs on the hookah,
a young man's thoughts can turn lightly to crime as a suitable occupation with which to impress mater and pater. In
this, as in all walks of life, great care should be taken to
ensure that the chap chooses the most appropriate nefarious
occupation, rather than plumping rashly for simply being a
bounder or a ruffian. Here, then, are a few suggestions for
those lawless careers that might appeal to the erring gentleman.

OPIUM SMUGGLER

Nowadays, sadly, the occupation of narcotics smuggler
has become the province of the common criminal and
even features on certain popular television programmes. Most of the modern malefactors even use
mobile telephones without shame. However, in certain
parts of the Levant the profession of opium smuggler
is still seen as one of the nobler callings, and after the
army and the church, remains the chosen profession

for many younger sons. There is no finer way for a young chap to acquire a suntan and learn the rudiments of azimuthal navigation than reclining on the deck of a dhow that is being pursued by the Egyptian coastguard. One should keep one's face perfectly shaved throughout, in order that the forces of the law will recognise you as a charming (though admittedly somewhat louche) Englishman and not throw you in prison for a thousand years. Those interested in this career should read Henri de Monfried's charming memoir *Smuggling Under Sail in the Red Sea*.

FORGER OF OLD MASTERPIECES

Even if found out, no jury in the land will convict a chap who has cocked a snook at the precious jackanapes who infest the world of galleries and art museums. There are few pleasures finer than strolling through the National Gallery and realising that all the Pollaiuolos and Poussins were painted by your good self one wet weekend last February. Selling the same painting to various millionaires from a garret in Paris is a pleasant way to pass an autumn, and the more people who want the original Birth of Venus, or Woman Without Clothes, the

more they will be prepared to pay. For this you will need to grow an exceedingly wild beard, wear a blue smock, consort with 'filles de nuit' and bathe only every four months.

GENTLEMAN BURGLAR

One must never steal anything so nouveau-riche as cash. One may as well attempt to win the bingo competitions that appear in the small-words-big-type newspapers, for all the respect this would bring you. Rather one should purloin netsuke, first editions of De Quincey and Huysmans, and Georgian silver candlesticks. A head for heights is necessary, as the self-respecting gentleman burglar will have to pass many hours clambering across the roofs and guttering of hotels on the Côte d'Azure. A gentleman's calling card is a must, as is leaving a few cunning clues for Lestrade of the Yard, such as a few empty wallets of After Eight mints at the scene of the crime. One should also become close friends with both the victim of the crime, and the detective who remains two steps behind. It is permissible to drop a few clues to the bloodhounds, but then to say, "Why how ridiculous, I could almost be describing myself to you" to your new friend.

ROULETTE SHARP

For this one really does need accomplices, clad in the finest dinner jackets that Jermyn Street can offer. Good manners prescribe that the chef de salon be informed that you are about to cheat the casino out of several million francs. Be sure to number among your accomplices some burly rugby players, just in case the sinister Italian count in the eye-patch takes offence at your good fortune and unleashes upon you some Corsican thugs intent on ruining the crease in your trousers. One does not, of course, resort to cheating, but simply takes the advice of one's chum who was a Senior Wrangler, and has devoted his donnish dotage to calculating a fool-proof system based on the Fibonacci Numbers.

GETAWAY DRIVER

Do not drive anything as vulgar as a Vauxhall Astra with go-faster stripes or a metal-look Nissan Sunny. Personally, we favour a 1930s supercharged Bentley in British racing green, with Vanden Plas coachwork and interior by Mulliner Park-Ward. If it was good enough for the 1937 Le Mans 24-hour race, it's good enough for making a clean getaway from the National & Provincial in the High Street. The more plebeian getaway driver will wear a stripy jersey and ladies' stockings over his head, but the gentleman will sport a tweed 'cheesecutter' houndstooth overcoat, motoring goggles, and string-backed gloves. A fine handlebar moustache will ensure that you sail through even the most stringent of police road blocks.

LOUNGE LIZARD

Although there is nothing actually illegal about separating a lady from her fortune, one should always wear one's cad's waistcoat in the pursuit of this. The aim is to appear to be a wealthy lounger, able to enter into effervescent chit-chat with wealthy ladies, preferably on their yachts in Monte Carlo. Express your knowledge of and interest in antique jewellery, and inevitably a lady will be unable to resist unlocking her valuables and asking your humble opinion (although this may take some time, don't leap straight in and demand to see them. Causes suspicion, bad thing). Express admiration, feign astonishment at how cheaply she values them compared to your expert judgement, and offer to have their worth verified by the

Marquis of Kidderminster, the famous amateur jewellery assessor. Hop off the yacht, antique jewellery in pocket, and flee to Blighty and the Lamb and Flag in Dover for a celebratory brandy and soda. Replacing the jewellery with fake glass beads is shocking form as the next fellow lounge lizard who makes the lady's acquaintance could waste valuable time in stealing these baubles.

POLITICAL ASSASSIN

However much one may wish to take an axe to the jumped up Oxford and Cambridge johnnies who pass for the government these days and cut them into tiny little pieces, this would be seen as an act of frightful madness and you would end your days in a home for Confused Gentlefolk, rather than be thought of as a true gent. It is perfectly acceptable to shoot wildebeest or Thompson's gazelles, but not to pot foxes: similarly in assassination one must always go for the slightly exotic and traditional victim. Shooting Balkan politicians is an agreeable way of passing the winter months. You may only shoot those that have been assigned to you by a man whose moniker is a single letter and who has an interesting scar on his cheek. A hunting rifle is the weapon of choice; however, one's trusty Webley revolver can be used in an emergency (evading Moldavian border guards, for example).

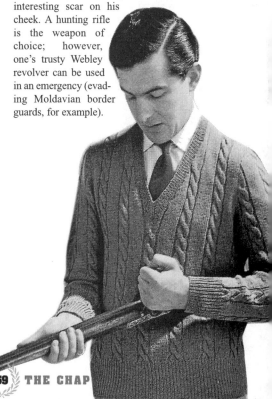

2002

£1.75

ISSUE

the CHAP

the CHAP

Jonathan Meades

Sweet Intoxicat'

The Ar
Good V

Da
Kh

MODERN ART

THE SPECIAL HAIR SERVICE

The Semiotics of Hea

A SUMPTUOUS HOOKA

UNFURL YOUR

3

CHAPTER

CLASSIFIED ADS

ACCOMMODATION

ROOMS OFFERED in shared maisonette in Pimlico. Would suit gentleman with broad mind and extensive smoking habit. All ancient conveniences, such as bidet, oak panelling, stained glass, mangle, Moroccan boyservant. Would suit non-vegetarian amateur. Timewasters welcome. Call Pimlico 341 preferably after midnight.

LONELY HEARTS

LONELY? UNATTACHED? Depraved? Assignations offers introductions to libertines. We meet regularly in a leather dungeon in Hertfordshire, and are currently seeking new members, following the recent demise of one of our founders in a freak cufflink accident. *Don't get trussed up alone – come and get tied up with Assignations!* Hertford 391

ALTERNATIVE THERAPY

EYEBROW THERAPY Disciple of Baghwan-Shri Roger Moore provides full initiation into this ancient system of mind, body and spirit development entirely through eyebrow movement. Call Felix Simper, Brent 243

ARTICLES FOR SALE

VARIOUS ARTEFACTS from Grand Tour of the Orient. Includes opium den, Chinese, circa 1894. Constructed in ebony, muslin and mother-of-pearl, this exquisite fixture can be assembled within the walls of the spare room. Comes complete with smoking hats and erotic figurines. Call Mayfair 437.

EGYPTIAN FACTOTUM, male, 14. This willing and eager little fellow is fully trained in most gentlemanly tasks, such as pipe-filling, letter opening and parlour games. Comes complete with small sack for sleeping purposes and riding crop. Requires feeding only once a month – box of Turkish Delight included in price: £120. Write to Sir Henry Spat, c/o the Reform Club.

PROFESSIONAL SERVICES

HAIR TRANSPLANTS. For those who find it difficult to cultivate facial hair, revolutionary new treatment from Sri Lanka relocates hair from the pubic regions to produce pleasing moustache and beard effects. For information pack, call Basil Singh on Croydon 254

FOOT BINDING For all your foot-binding and general restrictive needs, Madame Ling provides a comprehensive service. Call Soho 349

LOST PETS

LOST: UNFEASIBLY large Brazilian Anaconda, answers to the name of Trevor. Distinctive yellow markings and moleskin waistcoat. 8ft 7ins long, 10ins girth. Can be easily lured to safety by packet of polo mints. Please call Dundee 467 if cornered.

FOUND: POLITE male panda, 38 stone, with drink problem. Seems to enjoy being addressed as Cho-cho. Rapidly running out of bamboo and gin. Owner please call Cardiff 578

WHITE CUBE
✗
OAK-PANELLED ATELIER
✓

A FILTHY BED LYING IN THE TATE
✗
LYING ABED IN A FILTHY STATE
✓

PILE OF RUBBISH
✗
OBJETS TROUVES
✓

MIXED MEDIA
✗
MIXED DRINKS
✓

PRIVATE VIEW
✗
PUBLIC FLOGGING
✓

THE SAATCHI COLLECTION
✗
VERSACE COLLECTION
✓

MINIMALISM
✗
EXCESS
✓

INSTALLATION
✗
THE CONSTELLATIONS
✓

ANIMALS IN FORMALDEHYDE
✗
FELLOWS IN FORMAL ATTIRE
✓

SITE SPECIFIC
✗
THE SOUTH PACIFIC
✓

ABSOLUTE DROSS
CHALLENGING NEW DIRECTIONS IN CONTEMPORARY ART

CHAP ABOUT TOWN

Eugene Farquhar tries to unravel the mysteries of the contemporary art world

A rt has always played a significant role in the cultural and spiritual life of a gentleman. Many of my friends have found great solace in contemplating their Japanese watercolours bound in silk (sometimes while bound in silk themselves), or their collection of lithographs by Gustave Doré during moments of darkness, solitude and penury. An empty tobacco drum next to one's promiscuous briar during its enforced period of celibacy is enough to cut any man to the quick. It is during these difficult times that art can be a conduit for the mind to a more elevated plane – a plane of aesthetic buoyancy, a sort of aurora borealis of the imagination, where the spirit is free to roam among the elves, the fairies and the perfumed hyacinths of Arcadia.

This is more than can be said for the art on view in today's contemporary galleries. I took a hansom carriage down to Shoreditch, an area of London whose only previous place in my address book, if I may offer a little confession, was under 'H' for harlot. I had arranged to meet a friend of mine, aristocratic art pundit and titled beatnik Sir Matthew Glossington (or 'Matt Gloss' to his bohemian chums) in a Shoreditch cappuccinerie. He very kindly offered to accompany me on my peregrinations through the art world with a helpful 'insider' commentary on what we saw.

We entered a gallery called Grey Box in Hoxton Square. There was only one exhibit on display that day – the emptiness of the gallery indicated that refurbishment was under way, and the scruffy fellow in overalls who greeted us served to confirm this.

'Fridge' by Morphy Richards, consisted of a white, cupboard-sized hollow space, plugged into the mains, whose purpose appeared to be to keep things cold. On opening the door, as we were invited to do, one perceived racks of ordinary comestibles such as cheese, butter, milk and eggs. I turned to Sir Matthew with eyebrows quizzically raised.

"Ah yeah," he said, in his inimitable aristo-hepcat tones, "this is great. Look at the rubber edges on the door, old man. They're hip to a Bauhaus thing, y'know, moulded, chilly, recessive, stark. It makes you think about the whole crazy notion of keeping things cold. 'Are things cool enough?' this piece seems to be asking. Once your mind fixes on that, a whole host of fascinating questions pop up: What is the meaning of cool? What things do we want to keep cool? Milk? Sure, why not. How about butter? Hmm, wouldn't it get too hard to spread? OK, so how about eggs? What would a hen think if you suggested cooling its eggs? Major perturbation, I think you'd find, my friend. So, we finally conclude that at the heart of all this is a most perplexing question: Cool me down or shake me up, daddy-o?"

I thanked Matt for his helpful explanation, and we departed from Grey Box into the windy arena of Hoxton Square. Across the road, in the Luxus Gallery, a sign indicated that the building contained a 'major installation'. Disappointed, I was about to walk away when Matt informed me that, in modern art parlance, installation did not mean that repairs were being done, but was the name of a type of art itself. "Come on, old fellow, let's drift in."

'Flat', by Stirling Ackroyd, was an installation

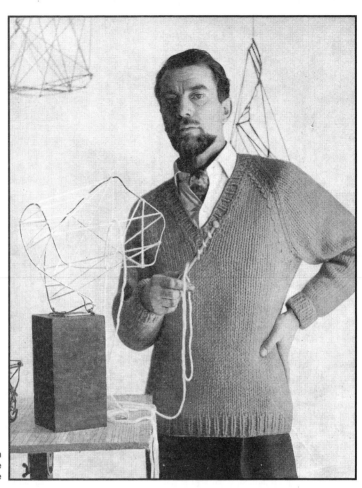

Sir Matthew Glossington
in his Buckinghamshire
atelier/thinking space

roughly the size of one floor of an average house. The viewer was invited to walk through four spaces of gradually diminishing size, the first of which contained large sculptures vaguely reminiscent of furniture, except they didn't look in the least bit comfortable. Compared to the exquisitely upholstered chaise longues and chester-fields in my rooms, these looked like they were designed for inflicting pain rather than pleasure. If I had children, which is highly unlikely, this is the room I should send them to for punishment.

Sir Matthew was more impressed. "I am immediately thinking about geometry," he said, his eyes narrowing. "Yes, this is a space which, merely by inhabiting, we are giving shape and form to. The layers of meaning become more apparent when we step through the doors, interrupting the

tyranny of emptiness." Say on, Matt. The next room featured a large sculpture roughly the size of a bed, but of a filthy off-white material more suggestive of a lunatic asylum. The floor was littered with clothes, empty bottles, make-up containers – the detritus of the young, I would imagine. Matt shared my eagerness to step through to the next room.

This smaller room featured several sculpted forms in white porcelain. Initially soothing, they gradually invoked memories of public lavatories, which I shuddered to recall. I asked Sir Matthew for his view: "This is very neo-dada. Duchamp would certainly approve, especially the collusion of properties – white, silver, polished, wetness." He approached a mirrored surface fixed to the wall – a mirror, in fact. I observed his face in reverse as he commented: "Looking inside, we see the outside. What is within is without. Totally gonesville, amigo. This is all-change-at-the-next-stop art, old thing, it's a runaway train that keeps coming into the junction and sends us hurtling on burning steel to somewhere else. I could spend all day in this place, and I might never get home again. Are you hip to what I'm saying, old bean?"

If only I were, Matt. Shall we go to the next gallery?

The next gallery was a much smaller, privately-run concern deep in the bowels of Shoreditch. Not many years before I had made regular visits to Madame Lafourge, a charming French mistress who had occupied the upper two floors of the very same building. Ah, what I learned from Madame Lafourge! But today I was here to learn about art, not about life. Sir Matthew led the way into the K2O Gallery.

We entered a small, damp cellar, with a concrete floor and exposed brick walls. A lone attendant sat in the corner behind a trestle table, reading one of the left-wing newspapers. She glanced up at us as we entered, and made some mark in a notebook at her side. I pitied her. The exhibit consisted of a single piece of work, mounted on a lone plinth in the middle of the room. 'Egg Carton', by Dairy Farms, was a species of papier mâché container about six inches by four. The top was open, exposing six identical oval objects in a smooth light brown material. I looked to Matt for guidance.

"Mmm," he said, homing in to scrutinise it at close quarters. "I was initially a bit down on the title, man. It's an anagram of Egg Art Con, but now I see where they're going with this. There is a sumptuous minimalist interplay between various abstract forms and surfaces – the playful roughness of the papier-mâché carton strikes an intelligent chord of dissent with the smooth sophistication of the six elegant ovals. One is transported to a 'space' within the imagination, fragile as the ovals themselves, sitting within an oppressive container which, while protecting them from harm, at the same time restricts them from freedom of movement . . ." Sir Matthew turned to look at me. "The Soviets?" he asked, not expecting an answer. He didn't get one.

It was high time for me to head back to my rooms and reflect upon what I had seen. I dropped into a bookshop to get something to read during the journey. My hand instinctively reached for a little tome entitled 'The Decadent Traveller'. A more appropriate title I couldn't imagine, considering the distance, culturally as well as geographically, from Shoreditch to Pimlico. I purchased the book and settled back into the Turkish cushions of my hansom carriage to leaf through it on the way home.

The Decadent Traveller, by Medlar Lucan and Durian Gray, whose very names conjure up a world of mystery, vice and *fin-de-siècle* depravity, is a document of their travels from Edinburgh to Buenos Aires, via St Petersburg, Naples, Cairo, Tokyo and New Orleans. I think you'll agree that, with the possible exception of Istanbul, these are the only cities worth visiting in the known world. At each destination the pair meet up with various Satanists, harlots and perverts, who lead them to the cities' epicentres of sin, ensuring that every pore of Lucan and Gray's beings is engorged with diseased satisfaction when they depart.

If the Comte de Montesquiou were to pluck a selection of books from the shelves of his library, hurl them into the arms of a travel agent and insist on being transported to every country mentioned therein, the resulting journal of his voyage would resemble *The Decadent Traveller*. In fact, one instinctively feels that many of these journeys were conducted within the confines of a well-stocked private library, where decanters of absinthe and an apothecary of opiates and hallucinogens share shelf space with the books. This is, I feel, is the only way a gentleman should really travel. *The Decadent Traveller* is published by Dedalus and is available, I am informed, from all good bookshops at the modest price of £9.99.

SIR,

I had just lit my faithful briar the other day when some frightful harridan accused me of 'invading her space'. Already banned from public places, pipemen will no doubt soon be liable for 'on-the-spot fines', and possession of a pipe will become a criminal offence. How different it was in the days of my youth! I well remember the occasion that led to my purchasing my first pipe.

Upon entering a charabanc I had seen two young girls who, while obviously of the servant class, were really rather pretty. I admit being somewhat miffed when they ignored me and gazed fixedly out of the window. Following the direction of their glance I observed a young fellow who, with an air of studied nonchalance, was filling his pipe and giving us the full benefit of his profile. "Oh!" Exclaimed one of the girls. "I do like to see a pipe, it's so manly!" This decided me to purchase a pipe immediately.

O Tempora, O Mores! Whereas one used to smoke in ducal mansions, rubbing shoulders with the aristocracy and discussing the merits of this or that tobacco, nowadays one is reduced to furtive sessions in the potting shed, while the gardener keeps a lookout for disapproving females.

MILES BURTON, HOVE, SUSSEX

SIR,

Whilst on the way to visit my old school chum, Sir Percival Bowles-Whiffing, I stopped to let some sheep cross and my Bentley flatly refused to start again. Having never darkened my gloves with motor-oil, I was at a loss to what to do. I therefore took to the lost art of hitch-hiking. Resplendent in my moleskin strides, brogues and Harris tweed jacket, I stood for a whole four hours! Many a lorry lumbered past, driven by foreign Johnny types who passed me looks similar to that given by Mussolini as the lamppost hove into view. Suffice to say, I arrived at Bowles-Whiffing's lodgings in sore need of several single-malt restoratives.

I have now taken into my staff a chap who can fix Bentleys at a pinch, using only a rusty nail and tweezers, who travels with me everywhere.

SIR BRODERICK STOOLS-BROWNING (VC, MBE)
BOOTLE, MERSEYSIDE

SIR

I write to express my utter contempt for the sneering and supercilious comments about Mr. Strangeleigh-Brown's letter (in Number Seven) regarding the inmates of our prisons as "absolute rotters", made by a certain Roger Brandon (in Number Eight).

The prison inmates described by Mr. Brandon as "businessmen, lawyers and accountants" are not Chaps at all, merely vulgar bourgeois excrescences for whom poetry, absinthe and opium are 'evils' to be stamped out in the unpleasant little conformist world within which they would like us all enslaved.

Let their footballer fashions crumple on their pustulous bodies as they lie incarcerated! Let their BMWs rust and rot outside! Let us sell their mobile telephones and spend the proceeds on foppish and exquisitely useless adornments of the finest fabric! Indeed, let their wives and daughters fall to our romantic pallor, our devastating charm and our impeccable dress!

Mr. Strangeleigh-Brown was indubitably correct in his assertion that prisons are "beastly places...full of...absolute rotters."

I REMAIN, SIR,
YOURS IN THE ARMS OF BACCHUS,
HATHERSEDGE TWEMLOW

SIR,
I was a little disappointed that you edited out the description of my bicycle [Questionnaire, *The Chap* issue 8]. I feel that, while falling off an Ordinary (penny-farthing) bicycle does indicate a certain lack of skill, it also demonstrates a willingness to try something different. Falling off an ordinary (modern safety) bicycle, on the other hand, shows sheer incompetence.

TED SEDMAN, PRESIDENT, THE HANDLEBAR CLUB

SIR,
As a man of humble literary ambition I am continually confounded in the writing of my journals by the lack of decent ink pens in our stationers. I find the crop of disposable biros and cheap rollerballs ineffably uncomfortable and quite inappropriate for the rendering of fine thoughts into crisp prose. The computer does not lend itself to ease of use when sudden mercurial thoughts grip the fecund mind. Besides, I do not personally encourage their use in the home when they exact such tyranny at the workplace.

Can anybody direct me to a prestigious purveyor of ink pens sturdy of body and handsome of line. Just as clothes maketh the man, so I feel the delineation of his signature discloses his true inner character.

EXCEEDINGLY YOURS,
ANDRONICUS CLENCH, BRIDPORT, DORSET

SIR
Seven Pounds Sterling (for a *Chap* subscription) seems a footling enough sum in this day and age. By the cunning wiles of happenstance, this is the self same figure required, long ago, to purchase that willow fruit of the labours of Messrs Gunn & Moore, with which I so singularly failed to distinguish myself upon the school playing fields. If I had a pound for every run I scored – well, as luck should have it, you now have a pound for every run I scored.

ROG PATTERSON, NOTTINGHAM

Sir,
This is the second occasion I have felt called upon to compose correspondence of a disparaging nature. The first concerned, of course, that ghastly debacle, the Second World War, when I was so put out by the whole charade that I wrote to WC himself.

Anyway, the most recent occasion I was called upon to leave the Horseradish Estates and environs (the first time in 14 years). I was obliged to brave the rigours of Public Transport, which I have discovered is best accompanied with a stiff G&T. Nota Bene: heavy on the G.

I was on the tram (with, I might add, no discernible rails or horse) in a position of by no means meagre discomfort due to the inadequacy of the upholstery and lack of soft furnishings, when I spotted a group of juvenile scruffs not wearing any recognisable school colours whatsoever. Upon accosting them as to their current social disposition, I managed to distil from the torrent of abusive cuss words and downright cavalier use of the English language a startling revelation, viz, that they were indeed pupils at none other than the old school to which I was prestigiously assigned: Haberdasher Askes. The aforementioned establishment is now nothing less than a (and I quote) "Comprehensive" or "State Institution".

Pray explain.

YOURS INQUISITIVELY,
WING COMMANDER HORATIO HORSERADISH
BA (HONS) MA CANTAB.

GIVING JERRY THE SLIP

Torquil Arbuthnot and Nathaniel Slipper's gentlemanly guide to surviving imprisonment in a German Prisoner of War camp.

This august publication has, even in its very slenderness, always attempted to suggest serious and realistic situations in which a fellow might find himself, and to proffer advice on the sophisticated, stylish and well-mannered course of action for dealing with them, whether this be coping with maiden aunts or even charming and dazzling the glamorous young debs. Continuing in this vein, the following humble offering will attempt to give guidance to the gentlemen who may expect to spend some time during their lives incarcerated in a Nazi Prisoner of War camp.

The first essential is to be captured in style. No desperate fleeing, no screaming ingratiating slogans such as "Churchill kaput!" and no being found up to one's neck in a pigsty (or even a pig). Rather, one should be found calmly waiting, with an almost-smoked Sobranie in hand. By merely raising an eyebrow you will communicate your surrender, but only after having completed the cigarette, showing that whilst you accept your capture, you will maintain your sense of decorum and not be rushed. You should, of course, be caught miles behind enemy lines, having completed your mission and selflessly allowed the other sterling characters of your company (Snowy, Ginger, Chalky, Smudger, et al) to have beaten the familiar path back to the Lamb and Flag in Dover. The only words of German you will need to know are "Hände hoch" (hands up). After this the enemy will speak the Queen's English, albeit in a clipped and sinister foreign accent. The correct response to this probably bellowed command is

"Afternoon, Fritzy, first class smoking compartment to Colditz Castle, my man", which conveys that, although you recognise your captor as the enemy, you will not be abandoning your manners.

On arrival at your new lodgings (as when you first moved into your rooms in Oxford or chambers at the Albany), there are certain members of the community it is advantageous to meet; and those who must be

Once captured by the Germans, maintain decorum by insisting on being provided with an operations room from which to plan your escape

avoided at all costs. You will, of course, be billeted in the officers' quarters, with like-minded gentlemen with whom you will be able to share tales of derring-do and high adventure. It is essential to be elected to the Escape Committee at the earliest possible opportunity. You should not intend to stay abroad for more than a month as colleagues in the Hellfire Club will be missing you. Although hoi polloi are usually to be given an exceedingly wide birth, here they can prove their worth. All of them will have pickpocketing and burglary skills, and some will be able to provide explosives, pick locks, forge identity papers, and even re-tailor one's greatcoat into an acceptable suit in Prince of Wales check. Certainly ignore the Poles: to them a stay in Colditz Castle will be luxury beyond their wildest dreams, and they will be far too busy trying to bag rooms for their friends and family to concentrate on escape.

Another fellow with whom you should certainly make your acquaintance is the Kommandant, whom you should treat as you would your opponent in a civilized sport such as backgammon or fencing. Show all cordiality towards him, accept his substandard port and whisky, even allow yourself a wry grin at his poor attempts at humour. You will probably be of benefit to him with your superior knowledge of culture, and be able to quote Shakespeare and Wisden at him, and show your disapproval of Wagner ("shocking stuff, goes on longer than one of Corporal Hitler's speeches, ha ha"). But never forget he is your opponent. Remind him of this at every meeting, and always leave him by saying, "I shall be leaving shortly, but I would like to thank you for your hospitality and shall send you a couple of Just William books on my return to Blighty." This will enrage him, and, in a particularly amusing Germanic way, he will stamp his jackboots, his face will turn red, and if you are lucky, steam will come out of his ears. Your coolness will mark you out as a chap amongst PoWs.

And so to the escape. This should not be rushed; nor should you simply take the first opportunity that presents itself of shinning over the barbed wire or jumping from the dining-car window of the 4.50 from Colditz. Far from it, you must escape in a manner that demonstrates your considerable panache and sophisticated awareness. For example, tunnelling through the sewers is no way for a gentleman to depart any lodgings, but is best left to the French, who display an aptitude and relish for this form of *nostalgie de la boue*. Not only is the digging of and escaping through a tunnel likely to ruin the sharpest creases in a pair of trousers (not to mention the elbows of a fine tweed jacket), but you are liable to emerge blinking into the daylight smeared with muck and filth. The natives will neither offer you assistance, nor will they suggest their daughter's bed as a place of refuge, if your appearance is that of a man who has just come from mucking out the stables. Give your support to the tunnellers by all means, aid and abet the supply of shovels, electric lights and gramophone records (the Eton Digging Song for instance), and even offer to stroll around the exercise yard shaking earth from the bottom of your trousers (a move known as "the Stalag Shuffle"), but when the time comes, a solemn shake of the head, "You go lads, my work here is incomplete. Now buck up, and chipper good luck to you all, and the Lamb and Flag on Boxing Day it is."

An elegant way of returning home is the nonchalant stroll through the front door. This needs little work, except for a German uniform and an excellent grasp of speaking English with a German accent. German uniforms can be hired quite reasonably from Ede and Ravenscroft of Cambridge, although you may need to pay a little extra to have one delivered in a Red Cross parcel, thus avoiding any prying eyes. Whilst speaking in a German accent, you will be understood and allowed to pass, although you are allowed to speak a little German, for example "Guten abend" (good afternoon), "Der Spiegelei ist rot" (the fried egg is ready) and "Mein Verkehrsampel ist kaput" (my traffic light has broken). Any more than this will arouse suspicion, and you will deservedly be thrown into solitary confinement. From here escape is exceedingly difficult, and you may have to cope with ruffian Americans banging repeatedly on the wall with their barbaric sporting implements. However, with uniform and accent intact, you can stroll purposefully through the main gate, bid a pleasant farewell to any guards, and can then travel peacefully by any means of public transport you wish, perhaps even procuring yourself a Mercedes staff car for the drive down the Rhine valley, until you step off the tram in Trafalgar Square. Be aware

> ## Tunnelling through the sewers is no way for a gentleman to depart any lodgings, and is best left to the French

that you will need a change of clothes if you subsequently require a peaceful evening at the opera, as the usher may mistake you for one of the chorus should you appear in the Upper Circle in the uniform of an Ubersturmbahnführer.

But for sheer exuberance and unbridled exhilaration there is only one way to go, and that is over the top and into the wide blue yonder. A secret workshop (a false wall in the chapel attic creates a healthy and holy space), 16-foot wings made from old bed-boards, a bathtub filled with concrete (or the collected novels of Mr W.M. Thackeray) and a couple of volunteers, probably from outside the officers' quarters with metal and woodworking skills, and within a fortnight you will be the proud owner of an airworthy glider. A pleasant spring evening with a comfortable breeze and you and your co-pilot will be away. A rowdy performance of *Blithe Spirit* in the camp theatre will mask the noise of your take-off. In this most stylish of ventures, it is essential to drop an empty champagne bottle through the Kommandant's skylight as you depart, who you would then hope to see hopping with fury and shaking his fist as you soar over his shaven head. Comrades cheer you on from the battlements and request messages to be passed on to loved ones, and a sturdy wind keeps your Cutty Shark of the Skies going; below the scope of enemy radar you ease home, with perhaps a swift dogfight with the Luftwaffe on the way. A peck on the cheek for the love of your life, "It has been rather a trying day, dear/Mother/Rover", a swift debriefing with the PM in the cabinet war rooms and finally a long evening with fellow escapees and the proud company of Mr David Hale, landlord of the Sonderlager Arms in the Haymarket, and his splendid cellars.

Miss Martindale

A rebuke oft levelled at *The Chap* is that we never interview any ladies. The reason for this is, quite simply, because there aren't any. Today's ladies of title, rather than cultivating colossal opiate habits and exotic foreign manservants, devote themselves to the twin vulgarities of mammon and public relations, while 'celebrities' of either gender clearly have nothing to offer *The Chap*. The subject of this issue's questionnaire, however, is the exception. Miss Martindale is a member of an all-woman empire of punishment known as Aristasia. This singular organisation, which was formed in the 1970s by students of Lady Margaret Hall of Oxford University, refers, rather accurately we feel, to the outside world as 'The Pit'. Aristasia holds various fundamental principles: the practice of discipline, both actual and non-corporal; the conviction that a matriarchal society is better than a patriarchal one, and the belief that the 1960s ('The Eclipse') signaled the end of the influence of femininity and the beginning of chaos. Discipline is a part of an Aristasian's daily life – Miss Martindale's maidservants are liable to feel the sting of their mistress's cane at any time. Miss Martindale feels that the female equivalent of a gentleman hardly exists in our language. "Lady can mean many things, and while it may at times carry something akin to the precise *nuance* conveyed by a gentleman, there is no real way of making that clear." The one thing we can be certain of is that Miss Martindale is, among many other things, a Chapette. Her remarkable life and work can be further explored by visiting **www.aristasia.org**.

1 Where do you think the best-dressed people are?

Mostly in the grave, unfortunately, but some are in the Graben. The Vienna State Opera still attracts some delightfully dressed people.

2 Which items in your own wardrobe are you particularly attached to?

My fur stoles. Several are delightful, and one can wear them in all but the hottest weather. One does like to wear a fur where possible. I realise that some people strongly object to furs, but even if they did not I think I should still wear them.

3 What single situation has been the greatest challenge to your wardrobe and your personal grooming skills?

Travelling on any form of public transport – a thing which I very rarely do, owing to the declining standards of the public.

4 Which view would you describe as a 'portal to poetic perfection'?

The Japanese regard the spring blossom as the finest of all artistic creations and accord it an almost spiritual significance. Looking out of my window in Baden Baden at the cherry blossom as I write this, I am inclined to agree with them.

5 What quality would you say has been the greatest benefit to your love life?

My looking-glass. I hasten to add that this is because it allows me to maintain a pleasing and elegant appearance – not because it allows me to behold the object of my desire.

6 What advice would you give to a young woman who aspires to being a lady?

She should acquire (I believe there are shops which sell such things) the latest copy of *Cosmopolitan* magazine. Read it carefully from cover to cover; and do the precise opposite.

7 Which aspects of contemporary life cause you the most annoyance?

Being a seceded lady, contemporary life is something with which, I am glad to say, I have little to do. *Positively*, therefore, it causes me very little annoyance. *Negatively* it causes me a great deal. The problem is not what it *is*, but the *void* it has created; the absence of a world in which one can live and move and have one's being outside a few select drawing rooms.

8 What vices, if any, do you believe are conducive to beauty of mind and independence of spirit?

Smoking, I think is one: but I am not sure that smoking can rightly be classed as a vice since it is a means to an end rather than an end in itself – the end being the use of one's charming cigarette case and delightful cigarette holders. Smoking is a performance, not an indulgence.

9 What items of clothing do you consider the height of vulgarity?

Modern "sports wear" worn for anything other than games – or, come to that, for games.

10 Who, in your opinion, is or was the quintessential English gentleman?

The English gentleman may take many forms. Lord Henry Wotton from *The Picture of Dorian Gray* is one form of perfection – unfortunately Wotton by name, wotten by nature, but we were not speaking of morality, were we? Another face is presented by Michael Wilding, especially in his films with Anna Neagle, most notably *Maytime in Mayfair*. If one does not object to a little *camp*, John Steed might be another choice. Such a pity James Bond was never played by a gentleman, or at least an actor capable of imitating one. And now it is too late.

PRET A PORTER

*In times of penury, the gentleman is faced with an agonising sartorial dilemma: to gad about during the summer season clad in last winter's heavy tweeds, or to face the ignominy of a ready-to-wear suit. **Sheridan Coxcombe** gives some pointers on how to survive the experience with dignity and panache.*

As every chap knows, the only decent suits you'll ever own are the ones inherited from your father, or those made by your tailor. Unfortunately not all chaps are blessed with ancestral wardrobes, and if one is short of lucre, perhaps after a disastrous racing season, then a new bespoke suit is out of the question. It is in such times of need that one may consider buying, if you'll pardon the vulgarism, 'off the peg'.

Buying ready-made clothing has much in common with self-abuse: practically everyone has done it at some time or another but few will admit to it in public. If, like me, you are one of the dozens (perhaps even hundreds) of debased chaps who have had to (or will have to) submit to the frightful ordeal of buying 'off the peg', be not alarmed, you are not beyond redemption. Indeed if you follow the advice I have noted below you may even succeed in buying a suit that, even if it is not first class, may not be the dreadful embarrassment you first took it to be.

A PERSONAL OBSERVATION

First of all, I would beg any prospective 'off the peg' suit purchaser to check the garments under consideration for signs of urine and faecal staining. At this point you might well cry out, saying, "Wait a mo! This fellow is off his rocker. Who on earth would buy clothing soiled in such a manner? Sad to relate, buying a soiled suit is an all-too-frequent occurrence. In four recent instances I myself bought clothing from a high-street clothier and subsequently discovered that they had been polluted in the most sordid fashion imaginable. I admit that on each occasion I was a little the worse for drink and did not notice their revolting state until after a few days' wear. However, I was refused a refund, and some of the staff made veiled comments to the effect that I had fouled my own clothing! One of the swine even had the nerve to set the constables on me. A scuffle resulted and there were (as nanny would have said) 'tears before bedtime'.

ELEMENTARY PRINCIPLES

So what are the elements of a good suit? Under normal circumstances a chap need only choose a good tailor and your problem is solved. You cease to think about suits at all and let your tailor proceed about his business, safe in the knowledge that any garment he suggests will be of top-notch cut and quality. Not so with the ready-made suit. Here you must inspect the garments on display carefully, and the wise will even consult small labels attached to the clothing to determine the fabric's precise content. While doing this you will learn many remarkable facts.

For example did you know that Tweed is merely a species of wool under another name? Extraordinary but true. You will also discover that some suits are woven of pol***ter. I need not say that no chap in his right mind, no matter how destitute he is, will wear any garment containing a shred, or single particle of pol***ter. A member of one of my old clubs once entered the lobby wearing a jacket that, as far as could be determined, was pure pol***ter. He was firmly but gently escorted off the premises, and has not been seen since nor is referred to in conversation.

THE FIT

Once a suit of suitable fabric has been isolated, it is time to judge its fit. For this purpose a number of

suits of different sizes will be on display in the high-street clothier. You could ask an oafish assistant to help you at this point, but bitter experience has shown me that you will not find the soothing touch of the qualified tailor here, so it is best to go it alone. Try on a number of jackets until you find one that doesn't make you sob openly or vomit.

How can you be sure the jacket really fits you? This is the very nub of the subject. Most chaps, in the absence of a tailor, would ask the opinion of their valet. However, should this trusty minion be out of the picture, try looking at your shoulders. On your jacket's shoulders you will see lines of stitching where the fabric of the shoulders and arms meet. This line should be exactly above the end of the flesh of your own shoulder, which should not extend beyond this line nor lurk behind it. Only an exact match will do! You must force yourself to try on jackets until an exact match is achieved.

Let us assume a match has been made. Your next step is to turn towards a mirror and examine the jacket's collar. Does the jacket collar ride up the nape of your neck concealing your shirt collar? Or does it hang low exposing your entire collar to the world? Neither situation will do! The amount of shirt collar visible must not exceed 5/8 inch or be less than 3/8 inch. Again, try on as many jackets as it takes to fulfil both shoulder and collar requirements. In the same spirit you must then examine your shirt cuffs. When at rest your cuffs should extend between 1/2 inch and 3/4 inch beyond your jacket's arms, no more and no less.

Next we choose the trousers. Your tailor would have agonised over the precise positioning of your generative equipment, the drape of your trouser legs would have occupied his waking thoughts to the point of distraction, and the fit of your waist would have given him sleepless nights. In the high-street clothier the best you can hope for is a snug waistband and trouser legs that don't end at mid-calf or flop over your brogues.

BUTTONHOLES

Incredible as it may seem, the quality of some jackets can be judged by the finish on the buttonhole. Normally a chap does not give this humble orifice a second thought, but a close inspection of this tiny portal can prove very revealing. You may even find that there is no hole at all, simply a line of stitching that gives the impression of a buttonhole. I hardly need point out that to wear a jacket deformed in such a manner is tantamount to sartorial suicide; old friends will cut you dead, waiters will stab you with hateful glances and doormen will dodge away at your approach. Should you ever be offered such a garment by a sales-person, no words are needed, simply show your displeasure by slapping their face.

Another breed of buttonhole is one where much of the correct stitching is in place but the hole is again absent. I know what I'm about to say may cause a shudder of consternation among some readers, but such a suit, *sans hole* as it were, can be worn in an emergency, but only in an hour of direst need. Such suits can even be made serviceable with a little surgery. The deft application of a razor blade can create a hole amidst the stitching that, at a pinch, will admit a carnation stalk.

PATTERNED FABRIC

Take your patterned jacket and look at the back. Examine the join that bisects the back of the garment from collar to rump. Do the stripes or the vertical lines of the check match up in a symmetrical fashion to form a series of 'Vs', or are they mismatched in a slovenly slipshod fashion?

Symmetrical lines will indicate that your suit has been assembled with reasonable care by the Oriental sweatshop workers who were engaged to manufacture it. Mismatching stripes will, on the other hand, indicate a distinct lack of concentration on the part of the machinist, perhaps as a result of giddiness bought on by malnutrition or a sudden attack of beriberi.

LINING

My final observation involves the lining of your jacket. I have fond memories of tailor-made suits in which the linings were of gorgeous, not to say dazzling, silken materials. A good lining should be exquisite and voluptuous yet discreet – much like a good mistress. It is your secret extravagance, only ever occasionally revealed by a sudden gust of wind, or the odd flamboyant gesture made with the arm.

Sadly your 'off the peg' suit will have, more often than not, a uniformly grey lining consisting of a suspect fabric that I have never dared examine too closely. Here your lining is not a beautiful woman to be secreted like a rare jewel, it is, rather, a deformed offspring to be hidden out of loathing, shame and disgust. The off the peg wearer is advised to keep his jacket buttoned at all times lest its frightful drab innards be exposed to prying eyes.

IN CLOSING

I hope my comments and observations have been of some interest. I suppose the moral of the tale is never to let yourself reach a position where such depths need to be plumbed in the first place. Still, it is best to be prepared for every eventuality, so I suggest you re-read this article and commit the more important points to memory before venturing into high-street clothiers.

I might also add that, no matter how much care you take in choosing an off the peg, you will always be found out in the long run. To put off this evil day do not attempt to wear your ready-made suit in polite company. If you must visit respectable haunts, adopt crepuscular habits, only allowing yourself to be visible, fleetingly, in the twilight hours. Avoid strong lighting, seek out the darker corners of the gloomier bistros. Scurry down side-alleys. Or join the clergy, whose clothing is subsidised. Above all, maintain decorum and dignity.

HOLIDAY IN ARCADIA We quizzed that louche old gadabout Septimus De Languedoc-Fizz on whether it is right for a gentleman ever to depart from the town of his birth. "Holidays," he drawled, taking a deep draught of his pint of absinthe, "are for the poor, the needy and the depraved. I therefore take one at least once a month." Here are Septimus's Dos and Don'ts of summer holidays.

SUNTAN CREAM
X
BRYLCREEM
✓

HOTEL ENTERTAINMENT
X
BEFRIENDING LOCAL YOUTHS
✓

SEAFOOD RESTAURANTS
X
STD CLINICS
✓

R & R
X
S&M
✓

PACKAGE TOUR
X
GRAND TOUR
✓

FLIP FLOPS
X
FLIPPANT FOPS
✓

WATERSPORTS
X
ENEMATA
✓

SUNBATHING
X
LYING IN A DARK ROOM
✓

SIGHTSEEING
X
PLEASURE SEEKING
✓

EASYJET
X
SLOW BOAT TO CHINA
✓

THE PELICAN CLUB
REVISITED

Brigadier Gordon Volanté recalls a most peculiar chain of events that occurred during a visit to his erstwhile gentleman's club.

I feel I must tell you of a most singular evening that I experienced last week. On Thursday, being at something of a loose end, I decided to pop across to Westgrove Belmont and visit the Pelican Club, an establishment where I had held membership for quite some time, but had not visited for a year or two. As I steered the Wolseley along the darkening country lanes, I recalled the chums who I had not seen since my last visit. There was Stephen Cavendish, a great ox of a man who loved rugger and fine ale, Dr Philip Greenswaithe, a fine batsman and the sort of chap who relished any form of high jinks, and Sir Christopher Hornsbridge, a barrel-chested sportsman whose trophy room boasted more endangered species than the entire Asian subcontinent.

I parked the motorcar and strolled to the club, removing my string-backed leather driving gloves and loosening my cravat, remembering with a smile all the rollicking capers the chaps and I had experienced over the years and looking forward to renewing these fine acquaintances. Imagine my shock upon discovering that the old verdigrised nameplate bearing the Pelican Club crest, which had hung by the entrance for as long as I could remember, had been replaced by a brightly polished plate sporting the legend, 'The Flamingo Club'! With a perturbed frown nestled beneath the brim of my jauntily placed driving cap, I stepped across the threshold and approached the desk clerk.

"Look here, my good man!" I declared with a sharp rap of the knuckles upon the polished mahogany counter, causing him to look up so quickly that his toupée flew from the top of his bald pate, flipped in the air and landed perfectly upon the marble bust of Sir Winston Churchill behind him.

We both decided to act as if nothing had happened. "Look here! I don't wish to appear boorish, but would you care to explain what on earth has happened to the Pelican Club, of which I happen to be a fully paid up member? Is my subscription still valid or not?"

"The premises have changed hands and certain memberships have been transferred, although all concerned should have been informed in writing." The desk clerk raised an eyebrow and looked me up and down. "Are you sure this is your kind of place, Sir?" he asked in a tone laden with cloaked implications.

"Are you trying to imply that I might not . . . fit in?" I murmured coldly, aware that my dress was a touch casual. The desk clerk gave a noncommittal shrug. I leant towards him.

"Now listen here. My garb may not be quite à la mode, but believe me, there's more to Brigadier Gordon Volanté than meets the eye! Be so kind as to check if there is a valid membership for me, for I am beginning to feel quite parched!" My little oratory seemed to do the trick. The desk clerk quickly located my credentials. I signed the book, checked in my hat and gloves, fired up a cigar and breezed into the club.

Something was most definitely wrong.

The atmosphere was correct, with a light haze of pipe smoke lending the red leather armchairs and potted palms a soft focus, the chink of ice against crystal and the rattle of backgammon pieces being gathered for a game.

But there was not a man in sight. The place was full of ladies!

I hurried for the sanctuary of the bar, which was thankfully deserted, and I ordered a stiff whisky and soda, noticing the barman's mild surprise at my attire. I made a mental note to wear an evening suit on my next visit.

"I say, bar-keep," I murmured discreetly. "Why on earth is a gentleman's club packed to the gills with fillies?" I found it hard to keep a note of outrage from my voice.

"You are a member, sir, are you not?" replied the barman in a confidential tone. When I replied in the positive, he continued. "Well, new club policy reads that Thursday night is . . . erm . . . Ladies Night. It seems that the ladies had been meeting privately for several years, until the club secretary revealed sympathies with their cause. The matter was brought before the committee, and it seemed there were far more ladies than was originally thought, and some of them in rather influential positions. As a result, it was decided that in this enlightened day and age a club should move with the times, and the motion was passed that Thursday nights would be allocated as, erm . . . Ladies Only."

"By jove, what a splendid idea!" I cried. "Why should the fairer sex skulk about in characterless drawing rooms when they have every right to taste the pleasures of same-gender camaraderie in an environment designed for just such a purpose! I just thank the Lord that they were not permitted to attend on the same nights as the chaps. One shudders at the thought of the depravity that would doubtless ensue!"

"I don't think that sir quite follows me . . ." began the barman, but he was cut short by loud voices as three fillies entered the bar area. "Are you quite mad?" boomed a well-made blonde gal. "Out for one hundred and twenty three after how many wickets? If you think for one moment . . . My Goodness!!" The face of the lady in question went quite ashen upon seeing me, and the pipe fell from her mouth. I bounded forward and caught it for her (catching an eyeful of a very well-made calf beneath tan stockings as I did so!). I gently replaced the curved briar between her cherry red lips and lit it for her with my Ronson, while I introduced myself. "Brigadier Gordon Volanté, at your service, ladies," I said. "Please, do not be alarmed at my intrusion upon your exclusive evening. I have just spoken to the barman, and he has explained everything, so allow me to say that I admire you, and think it very brave of you to lobby for such a controversial privilege."

The ladies looked amazed and relieved. "I came here tonight for a couple of snifters and some pleasant company, and I must say, it would be difficult to find better company than the three of you. Would it be dreadfully forward of me to ask that I might join you for an hour or two?" The

ladies readily agreed, and ignoring the barman's frantic attempts to attract my attention, I escorted my new companions to a table and instructed a waiter to bring us a round of drinks. I chose a Pimms, but the ladies, in keeping with the manly surroundings I presume, ordered flagons of foaming ale, which, upon their arrival, were guzzled with great gusto! Realising I did not know the names of my companions, I asked the well-made blonde to introduce me to her companions. She looked temporarily alarmed, before inquiring hesitatingly, "You don't recognise us, then?"

Puzzled, I replied, "Why, no. Should I?"

"Would you excuse us for one moment?" she said breathlessly, and the ladies hurried to the fireplace, where a rapid and rather heated discussion took place. They returned after reaching some form of conclusion and re-seated themselves. "You must think our manners quite dreadful, brigadier!" said the blonde. "My name is . . . Stephanie, and here on my left is . . . ah . . . Phyllis! That's Right! Phyllis!" she said, indicating her tall red-headed friend, who had just opened a rather elegant crocodile handbag and, reaching in, produced a large plug of mild shag, which she proceeded to tamp expertly into a rather formidable meerschaum pipe. "How do, old chap," she drawled smoothly, while drawing deeply upon the pipe, producing more smoke than a combusting barn. "Enchanted!" I replied.

"And next," Stephanie continued, "I should like you to meet . . . Christine." The lady in question seemed to choke slightly on a mouthful of ale, wiped the froth from her moustache, and said, "Bloody good to meet you, Gordon! Bloody good!" I took her hand to kiss it, but instead she shook it firmly, with a grip that turned my fingers white! The formalities over, we all immediately relaxed and chatted like old friends.

I complimented the ladies upon the way that gentlemanly traditions were respected by the female members of the club – all present were smoking and drinking furiously. An older woman flaunting an elaborate bouffant hairdo and a garish flower print dress also sported a sensible pair of Oxfords, with black socks and sock-suspenders. A lady in a fawn gingham twin-set proudly wore enormous sideburns and volubly berated a waiter for serving whisky that was "inferior filth", before downing an enormous tumblerful and demanding more. I did think they were taking things a bit far when, upon a visit to the restroom, I was shocked to witness five members of the fairer sex standing at the urinals, skirts raised, passing water and wind most volubly while discussing the form of the horses taking part in the 3.15 at Chepstow!

The night wore on, and all concerned became a little tight with drink, especially Christine, who seemed to be rejoicing in her new-found freedom. At one point, her moustache dripping with ale and her monocle steamed up, she grabbed my arm in a vice-like grip and declared most earnestly, "You must realise, Gordon, that although we may seem strange for wanting to do this, we are not perverts! It's not like we're into S&M, or anything!"

"Good gracious! Neither am I!" I proclaimed. "I wouldn't be seen dead in such an establishment! I have a tailor for my garment needs!"

At the hour of midnight I took my leave of these wonderful women, climbed into the Wolseley and carefully drove away down the road to Chipping Wimbledon, my heart warmed by more than just the volume of Pimms that I had consumed. That evening my faith in the female species had been renewed, and my old, jaded prejudices were rendered defunct. Here were women I could relate to, women who sympathised with the complex beast that is the chap. My eyes had been opened to myriad new possibilities, which might just include shedding the tarnished old skin of bachelorhood to which I had resigned myself, and perhaps indulging in the colourful dance of courtship.

In my pocket was a piece of paper, given to me by the wonderful Stephanie when I had told her how enchanting I found her, asking her to dinner at my home. She had blushed and batted her long eyelashes at me until one fell off, before rummaging in her handbag for a lipstick and piece of paper, upon which she had scribbled me a note.

On the front of the paper was the address of a vintage car mechanic. On the reverse, in cherry-red lipstick, was a phone number, signed: 'Your pal, Steve.'

PERSONAL STEREOPHILES
ANONYMOUS

Through no fault of his own, Phillip (not his real name) finds himself in the grip of a terrible addiction. Experiencing learning difficulties at school, Phillip fell in with the the wrong crowd and began listening to so-called 'hip hop' music. He soon found that his need for this barbaric cacophony was starting to get out of hand and he took to wearing that bane of civilised tranquillity, the personal stereo. After a very short time Phillip found that he was simply unable to function without it, wearing the infernal contraption virtually 24 hours a day and gradually pushing the volume slide higher and higher. He was hooked.

Today, at the age of 34, Phillip is hopelessly dependent upon his personal stereo. The damage he has sustained is incalculable. He now finds himself unable to hold a decent conversation and as a consequence has lost virtually all of his friends. He whiles away the daylight hours travelling on public transport involuntarily tapping his feet, sometimes blurting out disturbingly out-of-tune lyrics, and often proving highly irritating to old ladies. If you, or one of your friends or family, have similar problems and would like to talk to someone confidentially, please call Personal Stereophiles Anonymous on 030 767 556427 or attend one of the many local counselling groups. See local newspapers for details.

THE CRICKETING
CHAP

Torquil Arbuthnot and Nathaniel Slipper examine the inpenetrable technicalities of leather and willow.

As summer fades, the appalling intelligence reaches us, plastered across the back pages of newspapers, that many of our sporting professionals now face an entire season of wearing short trousers, shivering under bleak midwinter skies and sharing a plunge-bath with muddy teammates afterwards. Let us reflect, then, upon the dappled afternoons when we occupied ourselves with the only sport befitting a gentleman. Cricket, from a distance, seems terribly simple: one turns up, one plays cricket, and then one saunters off, feeling a sense of pride in one's sportiness and all-round good chapness. However, there are so many areas where even the most well-intentioned fellow, through naivety or ignorance of form, can be left departing the village green, shoulders hunched, with a sense of being a Bad Egg. Here are a few tips to ensure that you remain on the right side of the law of decent chappery.

EQUIPMENT

Never, simply never, have your own equipment, apart, perhaps, from an ancient, deep-sepia coloured bat, heavily taped up and smelling of fresh linseed oil. If offered the use of another more modern instrument, turn it down with a smile and murmur gently, "Wellington and I have been through too much for us to be parted now." Cricket bats should all be male and named after military heroes, or army or navy ranks (*not* RAF), or horses. Turning up with full pads, including bizarrely shaped ones that go on your arms or upper legs, or, God pity you, a helmet, gives the impression that you think you should be in the dressing room at the Oval, or the Long Room at Lord's, rather than reclining in a deckchair in front of a wooden shed in rural England. Small boys will throw stones at you, and they will have every right, both moral and legal.

BOWLING

If called on to bowl, a gentle leg spin will suffice. Bowling is a silent art and should be seen to be effortless; so no violent shrieks of "Owzat", no grunting as the ball is delivered, and no hopping around shouting "Catch it!" The South has now begun producing spin bowlers from the lower orders who mark out their run with a can of continental lager and a packet of Woodbines. Although this is to be secretly admired, leave this sort of thing to those to whom it comes naturally. Furthermore, you should certainly never ever attempt to bowl quickly. If the Skipper wants a fast

bowler he will go to the North and shout down a mine. Always show cordiality towards less well-brought-up team mates, saying, "Well bowled, Tyke" at every opportunity and slap him on the back when he takes a wicket. Do not expect him to reply to you, nor to indulge in idle chit-chat, because he will be tongue-tied in your presence and will be concentrating on wringing his cap and tugging his forelock. Remember, though, that the essence of being a gentleman cricketer is to be of the team, and not above the team. Any spectators should not be able to remember seeing you bat or bowl, but your team-mates will insist on buying your post-match Pimms and lemonade.

BATTING

When batting, one should aim mainly to retain one's dignity, particularly at the moment when one's wicket is lost. One should be half way to the pavilion before the umpire has removed his hand from his pocket, with perhaps a slight half smile and a knowing shake of the head. This will make the opposition realise what a sterling chap you are, and should encourage fine sporting behaviour wherever you play. The number of runs you score should be finely balanced so that you do not demoralise the opposition, or bore them as you slog around the ground all afternoon; but it should be enough so that your team mates will clap you on the back and exchange pleasantries when you return to the Pavilion. The following scores are recommended for each position in which one might bat:

1   17 (a "pantherish" or "tigerish" 17)
2   23 ("out before he could open his shoulders")
3   26 (known, in professional circles, as a "Ramprakash")
4   19 (a "Hick's dream")
5   22 (a "Pringle")
6   30 (this has to be a swift 30, no more than 6 overs allowed)
7   16 (always "a plucky 16")
8   10 ("like Horatio at the bridge")
9   8 not out (restricted to those born in Yorkshire)
10 3 not out (will always get the loudest applause of the match)
11 0 (out first ball – it is expected).

FIELDING
Certainly one should never try too hard when fielding. Allow yourself to break sweat three times at a maximum (but aim for one), and never remove your jersey or garishly-striped cap. On catching someone out, allow yourself a shy smile and toss the ball to the bowler at your earliest convenience. Transmogrify any congratulations into geeing the team up: "Come on, Old Satanians, up and at 'em," and such like. When fielding on the boundary, take a nonchalant, uninterested attitude to the game, smile at some of the ladies in their deckchairs, but never let the ball go past you as you gaze at a distant cloud. Do remember at all times, the ball is exceedingly hard. If it is hit firmly at you it will smart. Therefore, one must always turn one's evasive action into a seeming attempt to save a few runs. As it leaves the bat, move swiftly either to your right or left, and then as the ball hurtles past, lunge after it like a subaltern throwing himself on a grenade to save his comrades. Shake your head with a little disappointment and say, "Sorry chaps, should have had that one." Perhaps wince slightly as you limp back to your fielding position, so that fellow team-mates observe, "Poor old Biffo – the old war wound's still giving him gyp."

END OF GAME PLEASANTRIES
At the end of the game, ensure all hands are shaken, particularly those of the umpire. Have three drinks in the Lamb and Flag before you take your leave: a swift one with the opposition ("Darned

hard lines, old fellow, still there's always next year"), a half with the umpires ("No, no, no, you're thinking of Mountbatten in '54, that was the half century he made solely from boundaries while blindfolded") and your own team mates ("Why, thank you very much, don't mind if I do"). And then leave gracefully, fading into the blue twilight, with cricket jersey slung nonchalantly over one's shoulder.

If you listen carefully, you'll be able to hear both team-mates and opposition whispering, "No, no, didn't catch his name, but a damn fine chap just the same, and a first-class cricketer."

GENTLE MANLY REQUISITES

STYLISH MOUSTACHES

Bored of sporting the same old facial shrubbery day in day out? Do you wish that you could manipulate your moustachial manifestations on a regular basis? Ever wondered why Americans write 'mustache' when they clearly mean 'moustache'? Our transatlantic cousins may exhibit amusing idiosyncrasies when it comes to spelling, but they're certainly not to be sneezed at in the realm of time-saving innovation. 'Self Adhesive Stylish Moustaches' allow you to vary the hue and shape of your sub-nasal forestation, whilst at the same time bypassing the endless itchy months associated with facial hair cultivation. They also have the added advantage of being fully machine washable.

'Yessiree, go get those cotton-pickin' ladies, you hirsute rascal'

STYLISH MOUSTACHES, £6.50 inc p/p
from Mark Pawson , POBox 664,
London, E3 4QR
www.mpawson.demon.co.uk
cheques payable to M Pawson

HEALTH OF THE NATION. We sought the advice of that halitosed old rascal and septuagenarian necromancer Darcy Dandelion-O'Cruise as to some of the best methods of circumventing the horrors of the NHS, and transforming the onset of illness into a unique opportunity for personal growth and enjoyment. Here are Dandelion-O'Cruise's Dos and Don'ts of making the most out of a bout of ill health.

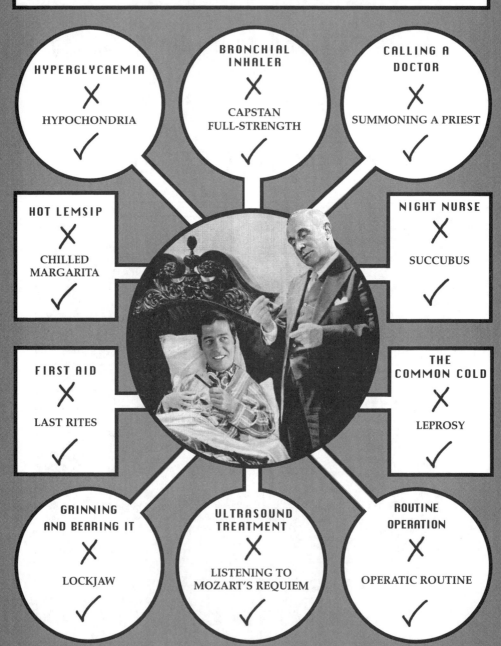

HYPERGLYCAEMIA
✗
HYPOCHONDRIA
✓

BRONCHIAL INHALER
✗
CAPSTAN FULL-STRENGTH
✓

CALLING A DOCTOR
✗
SUMMONING A PRIEST
✓

HOT LEMSIP
✗
CHILLED MARGARITA
✓

NIGHT NURSE
✗
SUCCUBUS
✓

FIRST AID
✗
LAST RITES
✓

THE COMMON COLD
✗
LEPROSY
✓

GRINNING AND BEARING IT
✗
LOCKJAW
✓

ULTRASOUND TREATMENT
✗
LISTENING TO MOZART'S REQUIEM
✓

ROUTINE OPERATION
✗
OPERATIC ROUTINE
✓

THE CHAP QUESTIONNAIRE
Jonathan Meades

Jonathan Meades is Britain's leading authority on the architecture of motorway service stations and the interior design of caravans. He is a vernacular gipsy on the highway of shattered illusions, a roving troubadour of folk-art cultural theory in the traffic jam of debut-de-siècle ennui; a peripatetic semiologist tunnelling his way under the gulag of contemporary human endeavour. Mr Meades also writes exceedingly clever and challenging novels. He is a Chap of the highest order, and we salute him.

1 What is your idea of complete sophistication?

Nabokov's prose. Schad's painting.

2 Who, in your opinion, is or was the quintessential English gentleman?

Alain Delon.

3 And the quintessential lady?

Monica Vitti.

4 Name your favourite three items in your personal wardrobe.

Black & Oxblood Spectator shoes by Emilio Blanco of Buenos Aires; steel-grey suit by Henry Rose of Dunhill; absurd disco-striped shirt by Hawes & Curtis.

5 What would be your ideal outfit for a day at Cheltenham Racecourse?

A horse blanket: mine is a grey Loden with green facings and stitching bought on site, ie in Nurenberg.

6 And the ideal outfit for a day at Ladbrokes Turf Accountant, Isle of Dogs branch?

A packet of Raffles.

7 Which view from which window would you describe as a "portal to sublimity"?

The view seen by the woman at my groin.

8 Where do you think the best-dressed people are?

Terence Conran's milieu/Torino.

9 What about the worst dressed people?

In general, the Italians: tan shoes with black suits? No!

10 What single situation has been the greatest challenge to your wardrobe and your personal grooming skills?

Buggery/cunnilingus/both – oh and fellatio when your head knocks the floor...how long have you got?

11 What items of clothing do you consider the height of vulgarity?

The lot.

12 Is there still a place for any type of moustache in our society?

The one that doesn't scratch; the one not worn by women.

BREAKING A LEG WITH PANACHE

Torquil Arbuthnot and Nathaniel Slipper investigate the art of treading the boards without the incumbent loss to one's dignity displayed by today's young thespians.

"All the world's a stage, and all the men and women merely drink a great deal, commit fornication and get up late" – Holinshed, How's About It, Act 3 Scene IV.

No-one seems to enjoy a more ebullient lifestyle than the actor. Fretting little and strutting oft, he makes his deep-voiced way from club to club, being lauded and spoilt by all he meets, having only to impart scurrilous gossip in return, pausing only to attend lavish awards ceremonies and entertain the matinée masses at the Royal Shakespeare Theatre every other Wednesday in the summer. A recent Oxford University survey revealed that actors have the highest ratio of agreeable claret consumed to actual hours spent at work than any other profession. So which is it to be then, a sober nine to fiver in an uninspiring cubicle in a dismal office in a building that smells of November, or the raffish, easy life of the actor, a life sans alarm clocks, sans cheap suits, sans commuting, *sans la vie en grise*? I thought as much. Step this way please...

So, how to enter this gentle world of Bacchanalian indulgence, pipe tobacco and languorous idleness? Unfortunately, the traditional method involves a year at what is laughingly referred to as 'drama school', where one will fritter away one's drinking hours pretending to be a panda bear, wearing ill-advised tight black clothes and ruining Mr Wilde's perfectly acceptable light comedies by setting them in a Siberian gulag, and having a skinny ginger fellow play Lady Bracknell in the nude. The only thing worth learning from these establishments is how to talk in a basso profundo voice, and this can be achieved without stepping foot in a 'studio' or 'rehearsal room', but simply by requesting Turkish cigarettes from your local Tobogganist. If asked one should always claim to have 'learnt my craft at RADA' – happily this can stand for 'Revelling And Drinking Association', 'Rum And Double Absinthe' or even 'Really Amateur Dramatic Arse', as well as anything else.

Yet surely one should learn the skill and the craft of acting? Of course you must. Happily, all the knowledge that you will need to pursue your new career can be gained from the tragic figure of Mr Dominic Leoline-Smythe, whose role in life appears to involve no more than standing outside the main entrance of these self-styled drama schools and bellowing, "You go on, you say your lines, you go off." A seedy vulgarian he may be, but a man of intimate wisdom of the theatrical arts (along with his detailed knowledge of the inner decor of most of the doss houses of central London).

The unsophisticated actor, armed with his acting knowledge and drama training, may now opt for admiring the reduced furniture in the finest leather sofa shop in Wakefield, wearing a scarlet and yellow dungaree combo on *Playaway* or appearing as a mutilated corpse in *The Bill*. If you too believe this the next step in the thespian career, then you should abandon this gentleman's quarterly now, and begin to affect a 'regional' accent so that you might end up in any of the penny dreadful soap operas that so occupy the minds of savages and peasants.

Priority number one must be the accumulation of anecdotes. Without a sprinkling of these glittering tales, people would tire of your three-page spread in the *Sunday Telegraph* colour supplement, let alone your company in Whites. One should begin with the one about Tom Baker and the crate of pineapples, and another about Googie Withers and Beerbohm Tree's wooden leg. On encountering other actors, one will immediately exchange these anecdotes, and hey presto, one has four anecdotes. Eventually one should have a mental encyclopaedia of

such tales, ranging from the wildly scandalous (usually involving John Gielgud) to the mildly titillating (Sheila Hancock, say, or Dame May Whitty). Also by taking part in this anecdote bazaar, one will make the acquaintance of and become known to other actors, with whom one can loaf for hours bartering tales. It is worth knowing that none of these fables have to be true, and that it is perfectly acceptable to change any names or incidents if you think there may be others more appropriate, or amusing. Always use first names or nicknames when referring to knights and dames of the stage. If in doubt, invent a nickname and precede it with an endearment; thus, "Darling Boffles Sinden" or "Dear, dear, sweet Stinker Dench."

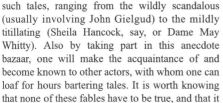

But the wealth, dear boy, from whence comes the wealth? There must, in your younger days, be some board treading,

and before one becomes too consumed with the gout one must occasionally perform the same performance daily and perhaps even twice daily, gruelling although this sounds. Happily, there are a number of parts that are crucial to the play, but take up little of your time. For example the Apothecary in *Romeo and Juliet*. Enter midway through the second half, a scene alone with Romeo, six lines, hand over the poison, exit, in pursuit of a beer. Three minutes of your time ensures a comfortable living. Each play will have such significant parts, too important for you to have to play another part, but not important enough that you must be sober for the curtain call. Whilst waiting backstage for your moment sous les lumières, you can rehearse your anecdotes for after-show imbibing, as well as picking up some new ones along the way.

And then of course, the film career, and Hollywood. Sadly all the great films have now been made, and rather than seek intelligence, wit or even a good story, modern films simply introduce you to rough ragamuffin creatures who will remove their clothes, drive too quickly and then blow things up, accompanied by needless profanity and the moronic throb of the 'soundtrack'. One staggers from the cinema trying to clap hands over eyes and ears at the same time. Thankfully, there is a shortcut to becoming a film legend, and that is simply never to appear in films. And not appearing in films by being too drunk.

When offered a starring role in a film, along with the fee, you will be offered all manner of sweeteners, perhaps a small Moroccan boy to sort your tobacco for you, or the use of a personal 'Jim' (whatever one of these mysterious items might be). Ensure your contract contains nothing but absinthe, vermouth, champagne (even if it be non Premier Cru), a man to mix you a perfect vodka martini, gin, Pimms, one bottle of Indian tonic water and one lemon. If you begin six hours before shooting, then by the time you stagger in to position, you will continue to stagger until you are in a position on the next film. This is also the perfect time to make wise amendments to the script (in *En Vacances, En Seine*, Matthieu Severiou's famous entry into the restaurant was such a moment, and the priceless look on Francesca Mangette's face is genuine). Perhaps swinging from the chandeliers, or emerging from the ocean in a white bikini? Happily you will be thrown off set until sobriety arrives. As long as you ensure it never does, you will soon be given a pleasant severance handshake and thrown into the next stage of the actor's life, the anecdotee.

Once an anecdotee, an actor is at the height of his powers, and will never need to work again. People will gather in huddles in green rooms everywhere to recount your latest adventure, before whispering 'No, really?!? Did Sir Ralph ever get the stains out of his waistcoat? Still, you've got to admire the old beagler, haven't you'. And on seeing you in the streets, erstwhile colleagues will propel you to fine eating establishments to harken at your denials, all the time adding the tale to their anecdotes, and exaggerating it tenfold the next time the tale is told. Likewise with fellow anecdotees, you should wrap up by a warm fire, ingest some vintage port and morphine for the gout, and simply laugh; words will not be necessary for you have partaken in the finest your profession can offer.

And so to the final curtain, and lighting the way to dusty death. The actor's death is unimportant, you could be run over by a milk float whilst dashing to the vintner's for a hogshead of sweet cider in naught but pyjama bottoms. The importance of the end is the reaction. The country should fall into a grief and wailing as if you were one of the family, as if a national treasure has left for that great proscenium arch in the heavens, and even the lights of the working men's clubs of the North will be dimmed in respect. And so the obituaries. A typical quote will be, 'he was always so alive, so vibrant', 'he wanted nothing but to bring joy and enlightenment' and 'but he was more than simply a fellow actor, he was a true and kind friend'. All that these kind and honest recollections really mean is that you toped a great deal and told droll and scandalous stories about people they knew. The lights may be dimmed, but your name will live on, and all for a grand total of no more than six hours' work in your twenties.

So leave behind the life of off-the-peg suits and cartoon character ties, market-ing projects and "dress down Fridays", throw off the veneer of the respectable working life, fire up a Sobranie, curl up with a splendid bottle of Bombay Sapphire, and turn to a friend, open eyed and hushed of voice, and enquire, "I say, did you hear about Julian Glover on the set of *Mason and Dixon*?"

SARTORIAL AGONY

David Saxby is the proprietor of Old Hat, a vintage gentleman's clothier in London where Savile Row style can be purchased with Skid Row credentials. Decades of dedication to sartorial elegance and panache have given Mr Saxby an expert and fastidious eye for all matters of gentlemanly attire and etiquette. In this regular column, he will answer the pressing queries on the subjects of cloth, cut, accessory and comportment that every right-thinking Chap should concern himself with.

Old Hat is at 66, Fulham High Street, London SW6. Tel 020 7610 6558.

I have been put forward for membership at the Reform Club. Any suggestions to help me secure a place?

Something drab to suit the rather musty ambience of the Reform. I suggest you focus your attention on getting into one of the more lively clubs, such as Madame Ping-Fok's in Shanghai.

When is it correct to wear a bow tie?

As long as you are able to make a suitable impact. It is important when wearing a bow tie to gauge the correct equation between flair and personality. It is imperative that your personality is not overshadowed by an ostentatious bow tie.

Is there a place for a slip-on shoe in a gentleman's wardrobe?

Yes, I have several pairs at the front of my own personal wardrobe. Slip-on shoes are ideal for making a speedy getaway from the boudoir of a married lady. Many good shoemakers create footwear that conceals a false side gusset. False Oxfords and brogues are very desirable, and the master of such things, and of all bespoke footwear, is of course George Cleverly.

How should one clean one's top hat? I have heard that Guinness can be used.

The quintessential silk plush for a top hat was mastered by a milliner in Paris many years ago. Sadly, he dismantled his loom in 1958, and the last proper top hat was made soon after the supplies ran out. If you are lucky enough to own a silk top hat, its upkeep should be approached with great care, as you would the head of a new-born baby. Clean the finish with a velvet pad, supplied when you buy the hat. The blackness can be restored by spraying the hat with Punch (brand name) Spray for velvet and nubuk. Guinness can be used, but not on the hat.

What clothes would you recommend for riding a bicycle?

A Norfolk jacket and plus fours, of course. Avoid as much as you can so-called specialist retailers, who sell synthetic cycling shorts of a rather louche nature. These do not really go any way towards flattering the physique of a gentleman, and as such can be left for adolescents or ageing interior designers.

2003

ISSUE 14 £1.75

The **CHAP**

**GLOBAL
CHAPITALISM**

The Semiotics
of Breakfast

HOW TO BE
A WAR
REPORTER

William
Bedford

The **CHAP**

ISSUE

SUPERMA
DRESSAG

AERON
ELEGA

DADA TUME

A Q... A PERFUMED I... THE BARBER'S SHOP ...THWARTED DESIRE

FILL YOUR BOWL W...

TOTAL SCARF

4

CHAPTER

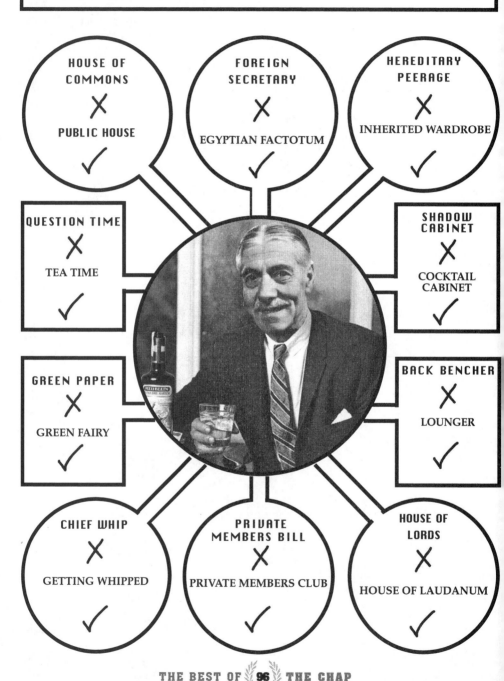

HOUSE OF COMMONS
✗
PUBLIC HOUSE
✓

FOREIGN SECRETARY
✗
EGYPTIAN FACTOTUM
✓

HEREDITARY PEERAGE
✗
INHERITED WARDROBE
✓

QUESTION TIME
✗
TEA TIME
✓

SHADOW CABINET
✗
COCKTAIL CABINET
✓

GREEN PAPER
✗
GREEN FAIRY
✓

BACK BENCHER
✗
LOUNGER
✓

CHIEF WHIP
✗
GETTING WHIPPED
✓

PRIVATE MEMBERS BILL
✗
PRIVATE MEMBERS CLUB
✓

HOUSE OF LORDS
✗
HOUSE OF LAUDANUM
✓

CHAPPIST DISPATCHES

Torquil Arbuthnot *and* **Nathaniel Slipper** *investigate the stimulating career of the war correspondent, and offer some Chaply advice on how to endear yourself to both the locals and your news editor.*

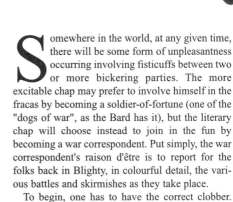

S omewhere in the world, at any given time, there will be some form of unpleasantness occurring involving fisticuffs between two or more bickering parties. The more excitable chap may prefer to involve himself in the fracas by becoming a soldier-of-fortune (one of the "dogs of war", as the Bard has it), but the literary chap will choose instead to join in the fun by becoming a war correspondent. Put simply, the war correspondent's raison d'être is to report for the folks back in Blighty, in colourful detail, the various battles and skirmishes as they take place.

To begin, one has to have the correct clobber. The non-chap will clad himself in a strange mixture of gaudy camouflage uniform and ethnic

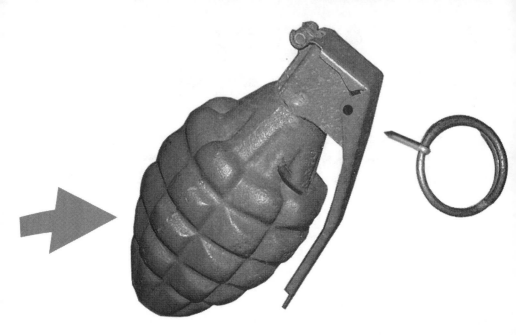

clothing, imagining he looks exactly like Lawrence of Arabia or some other such daredevil. The harsh truth is that he is more likely to be mistaken for the lead in the East Cheam Amateur Dramatic Society's production of Ali Baba. The chap should sport a thornproof tweed suit, stout hobnailed boots, a sola topee and a swordstick. This garb, with the addition of galoshes, will do for all climates. Of course your baggage will contain the necessary evening clothes and sporting apparel for those days spent dining or pigsticking with the British Ambassador. An essential part of the war correspondent's apparel is a picturesque war wound. This can be accomplished by affecting a slight limp and muttering, "Copped a ricochet at Dién Bién Phû," or "Curse that Biafran sniper."

Much of the war correspondent's life is spent wandering the countryside, following warring armies from roughhouse to roughhouse. Therefore you should travel light: limit your retinue to the bare essentials. Around twenty-five servants (not counting native bearers, guides, nautch girls) should suffice if one is roughing it (valet, "tiger", ostler, postillion, chef, sous-chef, boy who does the boots, string quartet, etc). Similarly one should restrict one's baggage to the bare necessities of life, and take no more than would fit onto seventeen or eighteen packhorses: Corby trouser press, half-size billiards table, collected works of Mr George Orwell, collapsible flagpole, jeroboam of port, set of golf clubs, baby grand piano, pack of beagles, etc). The noble British pound is sadly not accepted in certain far-flung parts of the world, therefore one cabin trunk should be reserved for local currency and gifts for the natives: krugerrands, cassette tapes of Ms Doris Day (the correspondent's sweetheart), windscreen wipers, jars of Marmite (common currency in Madagascar), and, of course, back copies of *The Chap*.

Upon arriving abroad, ignore the jumped-up pen pusher at Immigration who demands to see your passport. Explain to him that passports are for hobbledehoys who holiday in vulgar sunspots like Torremolinos and Rhyl, and flourish a copy of *The Chap* while bellowing, "Official war correspondent (seconded from the etiquette pages)." It is also a good idea to show the nearest uniformed and bemedalled flunky a photograph of yourself at Oxford with "el Presidente". This will get you past the most stringent border controls.

The vulgar war correspondent will then hole up in the local Hyatt Regency. The chap will, of course, be blood brother to every dacoit and brigand 'twixt Novya Zemla and Tierra del Fuego, and will enjoy the hospitality of the local warlord or bandit-chief. This personage will provide suitable bearers, guides and nautch girls. He will also provide, if absolutely necessary, an interpreter. As is well known, all foreigners speak perfect English behind one's back but jabber in outlandish tongues in front of one merely out of affection. It is best to humour them. Besides, the classically educated chap will have a smattering of most such outlandish tongues, such as Xhosa, Farsi, Tagalog, Targui, Inuit and Welsh.

Most war correspondents will communicate their missives back to the news desk via some chromium-plated vulgarity such as the "video phone" or the "satellite link". The chap will not bother with such modern fripperies, but will employ such tried and tested means as the runner with his cleft stick, the noble balloonist, the brave carrier pigeon, the heliograph, or the bulletin tattooed on a messenger's bald head (once the hair grows back the messenger is dispatched to London, where the news editor shaves his head to read the message).

As to the tedious business of reporting the various brawls and altercations, begin each article with the words, "As the bullets whizzed/sang/ripped/buzzed over my head..." Lace your account with plenty of local slang and military argot ("Shabash! shouted the *sin camisa* as the Cherrypickers started to stonk the sangar"). Should there be a cease-fire, it is perfectly permissible for the war correspondent to ginger things up a bit by lobbing grenades in all directions until the shooting restarts, or pass messages of hostile intent from one side to the other.

Of course the sensible chap will not bother with all the folderol and disagreeableness of travelling abroad and being sniped at. The nearest he will come to the savage land of Abroad will be the snug of the Lamb and Flag at Dover, a brandy-and-soda at his side, and write colourful "dispatches from the front" with the aid of a schoolboy atlas, the Observer Book of Things That Go Bang and the 1907 Baedeker Handbook for Bechuanaland.

Howard Spent investigates

THE SEMIOTICS OF BREAKFAST

To the man on the street, a man of bland psyche and limited imagination, the concept of 'breakfast' will not be regarded as worthy of a jot of philosophical cogitation. However, to a trained semiologist, the very roots of the word open up a complex web of contradiction and intrigue.

Take, if you will, the idle boast of the haughty super-model or the hyperactive New York trader that they usually 'skip breakfast'. The sorry implication of such a claim is that they are either too 'body aware' or, simply, too busy to indulge in such a luxury. But to a man of linguistics it is immediately apparent that whilst it is conceivable to postpone breaking one's fast it is not something that can be 'skipped' or put off indefinitely. Unless one is unfortunate enough to be a dedicated anorexic, a famine victim, a political prisoner on hunger strike or some species of speciality monk, at some point in any period of 24 hours it becomes very pressing indeed to call off the 'fast' and 'break' into the comestibles with élan.

Whether breakfast is consumed by an ill-hewn farmer at some ungodly hour of the morning or by a decadent fop in the mid-afternoon it still remains recognisably and incontrovertibly 'breakfast'. Judging by the plethora of taverns and inns boasting that they serve 'all-day breakfasts' the definition of this pivotal meal of the day goes a long way beyond the mere time of its consumption.

Of one thing we can be certain. One hungry fellow's petit dejeuner is another's dog's dinner. The array of so-called breakfast items is as vast and varied as species of tree frog in the lower Congo Basin, and as one travels about the globe one realises that there is no common sensibility that governs how a fellow should tackle the tricky business of 'the most important meal of the day'. What may be deemed a perfectly reasonable menu choice in Ulan Bator is highly unlikely to meet with very much approval with the residents of the Ball's Pond Road.

It soon becomes clear that we have opened up quite a can of worms. 'Breakfast' is obviously a moot metaphysical concept of some complexity. Its definition neither relies solely on the fast-breaking intentions of the eater, its time of consumption, nor the type of nutrition that is consumed. This is what makes it an ideal implement for the semiotician. How each and every one approaches the inaugural nosebag of the day may tell more than we would wish to reveal about our temperament, social standing and financial affairs.

Dear reader, I have spent the previous three months touring transport cafés, bijou tea shops, five-star hotels and continental brasseries across the land, shovelling vast quantities of nutrient down my oesophagus in pursuit of the 'truth'. I have observed at first hand the intimate breakfasting habits of the populace and gained startling insight. Although I have limited my investigations to the United Kingdom, I think you will agree that the variety found in our own small islands is by far enough to occupy the limited room at our disposal.

So, study and memorise the following pages, and then step out onto the public arena and track down the specimens illustrated. With a keen eye and some patient observation, I'm sure you'll find the semiotics of breakfasts an invaluable aid for use socially, in business and for pleasure.

The Hasty

The unseemly pace of modern commerce can lure 'dynamic' business types into skimping on their morning repast. The sallow and pitiful comestible known as the nutri-snack is nature's way of punishing a soul mired in the pursuit of Mammon.

The Civilised

As impressive as a Gieves and Hawkes suit or a full hand in a game of Baccarat, the full English breakfast remains the hallmark of a cultivated fellow with buckets of time on his hands and the sacred song of Orpheus in his heart.

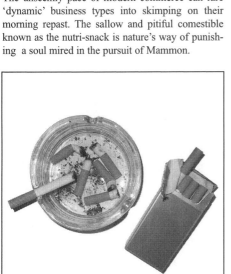

The Inspiring

The concept of the *liquid lunch* is very much established in London journalistic circles, but the less familiar *fumatory breakfast* goes down a storm with struggling artists and poets. A tobaccic start to the day can only be regarded with admiration and awe.

The Unhealthy

There is a wrong-headed notion that regards the consumption of fruit and nuts as in some way desirable and impressive. Such degrading behaviour has been rumoured to lead to 'postmature youthing'. The sickly cult must be reviled and expunged.

The Restorative

Losing one's family fortune on some ill-judged speculation on equine variables is a laudable hobby for any young man of thrust and daring. The noble Martini can act as a much-needed anaesthetic prior to a morning business meeting with one's turf accountant.

The Invigorating

Nothing can quite compare to the stimulating effects of an early morning enema. A jaded aesthete may find himself so consumed with languidity and inertia that he loses the capacity to chew, and must adopt alternative methods of absorbing nutriment.

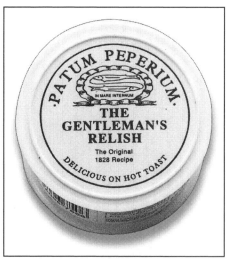

The Sublime

A fellow prone to spiritual ecstasy and transcendentalism will break his fast with toast delicately spread with Patum Peperium. Less of a comestible and more of a blessed sacrament, this exquisite relish anoints the late riser with the blessed balm of Poseidon.

The Vulgar

My God, what knavery is afoot here? This dreadful thing almost seems to be grinning at us! No fellow worth the epithet of gentleman would deign to pollute his physique with an ersatz egg sandwich purchased from a High Street fast-food outlet.

The Continental

Although it bears a fleeting resemblance to a romantically-charged lunar manifestation, the croissant should be given very short shrift. Gallic posturing in the realm of the kitchen and the bedchamber can sometimes make an Englishman's blood run cold.

The Erotic

A lothario impatient to make the acquaintance of cultured ladies in his area could do worse than start the day with oysters. Inordinate consumption of this feisty bivalve is guaranteed to cement his prominence as an upstanding member of the early music society.

The Meagre

Some may think that the 15th Earl of Camardenshire's penchant for ladies' clothing singles him out as a perverse scion of a noble line, but nothing damns him quite so surely as his slavish adherence to the slimming tips he finds in the pages of *Cosmopolitan*.

The Satanic

Selling one's immortal soul to Beelzebub has long been a valid option for a gentleman wishing to remain youthful or to side-step pressing gaming debts. Consuming devilled kidneys naked, at dawn, on the winter solstice is tantamount to signing the contract.

GLOBAL CHAPITALISM

HAIR STEWARD

Indian Airlines employee wins legal battle to keep handlebar moustache

An air steward with Indian Airlines won legal action against his employer against being grounded because of his prominent handlebar moustache. Victor Joynath De's moustache did not conform to airline regulations and he had ignored repeated warnings to trim it. Mr De, 56, said he was proud of his moustache, which took 25 years to grow and stretches prominently across both cheekbones. "I never dreamed of trimming it," he says. "In the 33 years I have worked for the airline, my moustache has attracted many adoring eyes inside the plane and on the ground."

But Indian Airlines argued that his prized asset was a health risk, especially as he frequently handles food. Mr De was grounded and reduced to doing a desk job at Calcutta airport dealing with passenger complaints.

He promptly filed a writ petition in the high court, claiming that growing a moustache was his fundamental right. Indian Airlines' defence was that a staff circular had clearly stated that a steward's moustache must be 'neat and trim' and must not grow beyond the upper lip. But lawyer

Arunava Ghosh, a former secretary of the Bar Association of Kolkata, says that the airline cannot single out Victor when Sikh stewards are permitted to grow their hair, beard and moustache without any restrictions.

A victorious Victor Joynath De leaves the court

The Chap is delighted to announce that that Mr De won the case, and in February was reinstated as an air steward, with his magnificent handlebar still intact.

The Handlebar Club of Britain was of course delighted to hear about this glorious victory. Its president, Ted Sedman, said: "One of our members, a San Francisco policeman, had the same problem a few years ago. He took his employers to court and won — I think it was on the grounds of sex discrimination!"

HIP FOP GENERATION

Rap chanteur shows interest in gentlemanly tailoring with new clothing line

The American 'rapper' known as Puff Daddy—who has opted for a seemingly pointless name change to P Diddy—has launched a new collection of clothes that has its roots in the English Savile Row style. Mr Diddy's clothing line, Sean John, presented its autumn/winter 2002 collection at the Cipriani ballroom in mid-town New York in February.

> "YOU CAN OPEN DOORS FOR WOMEN AND LOOK AFTER THEM AND STILL BE A POWERFUL DUDE."

Mr Diddy's previous collections have tended more towards what is known among the hip-hop generation as 'ghetto fabulous', and consisted primarily of jeans, vulgar jewellery and plimsolls. There were even rumours of embarrassingly expensive trousers made of mink — clearly a sartorial nod towards those lovably mischievous 'characters' that Mr Diddy is known to associate with. The new collection, in contrast, shows remarkable taste, being entirely constructed of fabrics such as tweed, corduroy, wool plaid, velvet and cashmere. Mr Diddy was apparently spotted last year in the environs of Savile Row, from where he is said to have drawn inspiration.

The Chap would like to remind readers that Savile Row, as well as housing the best tailors in the land, is also home to a rather busy police station.

The Chap must, however, concede that any step in the correct sartorial direction is to be welcomed, and we were most taken by the reports of brown wool pinstripe three-piece suits, grey and blue windowpane check suits with white dress shirts and striped old school ties; the models also carried fob watches and pocket handkerchiefs. The English gentleman was further suggested on the catwalk by the use of British ex-public schoolboy (Sherborne, but there it is), Jamie Strachan, as a model.

Mr Diddy himself was eager to promote his new-found love for gentlemanly ways, and had clearly been cognisant of the spread of Chappism. "It's time to bring back the gentleman," he said. "You can open doors for women and look after them and still be a powerful dude."

The Chap performs a complicated hand gesture and gives a big 'Huzzah!' to the P Diddy massive.

HIP REPLACEMENTS

A novel solution to the ladies' lack of girth in the pelvic department

An alarming number of young ladies these days appear to have lost control of their waistbands. It has become a common sight upon the public thoroughfares of our towns to observe a little too much of a lady's undergarments, as the waistband of her trousers struggles to maintain its correct position somewhere in the small of the lower back. To the gentleman observer this can be the cause of some distress, for he only considers it proper to examine the undergarments of those ladies who have promised themselves to him in a sexual capacity. Peer pressure to maintain a physique more redolent of a lithe Spanish waiter than a fecund child-bearer is one factor contributing to this malady, as well as a poor diet and poorly constructed legwear. Today's young lady would appear to be consigned to a life of constantly hitching up her pantaloons, and not having any control over precisely who might be cognisant of the colour of her underwear. Until now, that is.

The Hip Replacement, by Torniquet & Blanche, is a novel way to boost a lady's inadequacies in the pelvic department. The two pads are slipped into the trousers at hip level, thus rendering the pelvis of an adequate curvature to support the most flimsy of legwear. The Hip Replacements come in three sizes, with a choice of white, salmon pink or blue. They come in packs of two, so one pair can be worn while the other pair slips conveniently into the handbag. £2.99 from all good haberdashers.

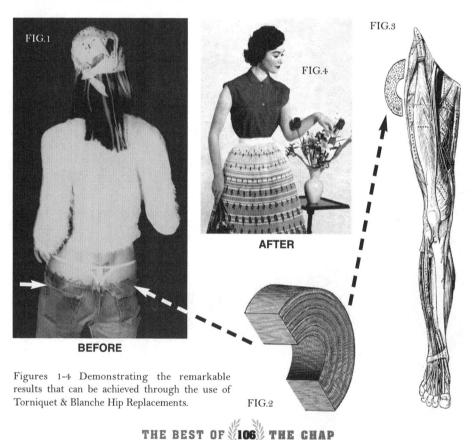

FIG.1

FIG.3

FIG.4

AFTER

BEFORE

FIG.2

Figures 1-4 Demonstrating the remarkable results that can be achieved through the use of Torniquet & Blanche Hip Replacements.

DRESSING GOWN FRIDAY

Sherwood Pimlico finds that, with a little imaginative use of ergonomics, working at home can be almost as pleasant as not working at all.

One of the first principles of the Chap way of life is to maintain complete elegance and panache at all times, in every activity. Thus we will always try, as far as possible, to avoid any form of work at all, preferring the dignity of penury to the ignominy of slavery. However, when it does occasionally become incumbent upon us to replenish our coffers in the grand marketplace of human misery, we choose careers that needn't disturb the tranquillity and harmony that we have created within the sacred oak-panelled walls of our rooms. Such occupations might include book reviewer, poet, wine journalist or limerick writer.

One of the details that appears to fascinate many people who work from home these days is the rather tiresome matter of office furniture and ergonomics. After a decade of nine-to-five, office workers who are released into the wild paradoxically celebrate their freedom by constructing elaborate labyrinths of MDF, moulded plastic and fibre-optic cable in their two-bedroom flats in Hounslow. A whole industry is now devoted to the manufacture of the sort of furniture that would result if Antonio Gaudi had been forced at gunpoint to design a new range for Ikea. The 'home workers', as they dub themselves – in a chilling evocation of childhood evenings chained to a desk with an exercise book and a volume of Latin verbs – then ensconce themselves in their high-tech nests, expecting to be somehow camouflaged from the rest of the household. *The Chap* would argue that, in attempting to fool themselves and their families that the humble dining room is in fact a modern office where important things happen that affect the real world, these home workers have in reality thrown out the baby with the bathwater.

There is really no need for all this DIY jiggery pokery, because the ideal office space is right under one's very nose – the bed. What item of furniture could embody the science of ergonometry more beautifully than the double bed? Everything can be placed within easy reach; there is plenty of room to spread out (far more than your average desk, assuming sole occupancy of the bed during office hours), and, above all, there is comfort. Expensive office furniture is all very well, but how on earth is one to have a quick snooze while hunched over a computer keyboard in the corner of the kitchen? When working in bed it is easy – simply drop your fountain pen, push your documents aside and sink back into the pillows with a languorous sigh.

To refine your working environment, there is much that the sophisticated home worker can learn from the hospitalised invalid. Certain configurations of pillows can be created to maintain comfort throughout a 24-hour period of residence in one's bed. Bowls of fruit make a nice centrepiece for the bedside table, and provide pleasant snacks while leafing through a novel one has been asked to review. The advantage that the home worker has over his invalid counterpart is of course space. While most hospitals believe that a single bed meets every patient's requirements, we would be unwise to follow this practice. A double bed provides ample space for books, documents, stationery, food trays, a telephone, bottles of gin, dictionaries, atlases, bibles, the complete works of Shakespeare, and any other essential requisites for those immersed in the world of belles lettres. If one's personal secretary is required to take a letter, get him to perch comfortably on the corner of the bed while you dictate it.

This brings us to the subject of staffing your home office. This is an area too often neglected by today's home workers, to their great detriment. If a modern office is run by a complex hierarchy of MDs, executives, middle management, PAs and press officers, why the devil should a home worker expect to manage his housebound office single-handedly?

It is clear that we would be far more efficacious working machines if able to delegate responsibility to the appropriate member of staff. *The Chap* recommends the following basic stable. One personal assistant, for basic errands such as going to the shops for more Martini, placing bets at the turf accountant and so forth; one secretary, for letter writing, phone calls, and liaising with the family to ensure you are not disturbed; one financial adviser, to co-ordinate expenses and fiddle your tax return; and one PR guru, to ensure you maintain a decent profile within the community. Neighbours can become very suspicious of people who never leave the house, imagining them to be involved in something sinister to do with the Internet, or, even worse, unemployed. Your PR guru can get you a seat on some local committee or other, and get a few stories in the local newspaper about your sterling work in helping old ladies across the road.

A final note on dress. One of the luxuries of home working is that every day is dress-down Friday. You can take this a step further by not getting dressed at all, and spending the entire day in your bedclothes. For the men, a nice pair of brushed cotton pyjamas, a silk dressing gown and a pair of monogrammed velvet slippers are ideal. The ladies can spend all day sheathed in Chinese silks far too expensive to wear outside the house, and enjoy the sadly neglected delights of the bed coat. This splendid woollen garment maintains an even temperature on the arms and shoulders, while permitting the erratic flourishes of the professional writer's pen.

Consider it the height of professional achievement if, come six o'clock in the evening, you are enjoying your second gin and tonic of the day while still dressed for bed.

SUPERMARKET
DRESSAGE

Elliott Fairweather reins in his trusty steed, hones his equestrian skills and prepares to impress the ladies.

T he perennial problem of locating and wooing a suitable mate has not been made easier over recent years by a growing culture of urban isolation. Today's young men and women increasingly live on their own, only venturing out of their abodes to cater to the filthy dictates of office, night club or gymnasium. The Chap who finds all three of these environments thoroughly reprehensible may find that modern mores are turning his quest for love from an invigorating challenge into an almost insurmountable chore.

If we are to believe the newspapers (and there is no earthly reason why we should) some of today's most fertile arenas for making the acquaintance of members of the opposite sex are art galleries and supermarkets. The former will come as little surprise to a fellow of quality, well versed in the arts, who often finds himself so overcome by Titian's 'Death of Actaeon' in the National Gallery that he is prone to spontaneously weeping on the shoulders of total strangers. Such airing of passions is guaranteed to go some way to breaking the ice. But could anyone regard the bleak sterility of the supermarket as in any way conducive to the requirements of Eros? Well, apparently so.

As odd as it may seem, a goodly amount of ladies of impeccable breeding are to be found in these halls of commerce and if a bevy of tweedy young women are there to be met, then an ardent young gent should be prepared to travel to the ends of the earth to meet them.

'But,' you may ask, 'how is a fellow to flaunt his chappist credentials in such a place?' The answer is simple. A new code of gentlemanly display is currently catching on amongst those in the know,

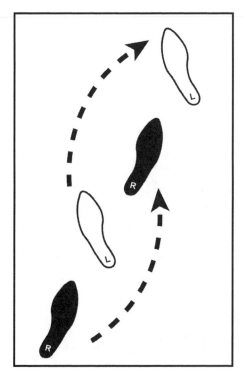

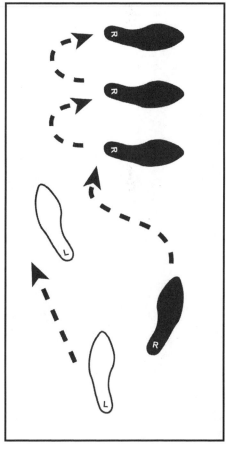

Fig 1. Correct steps for a 'trot zigzag half-pass' performed in the frozen fish section.
Fig. 2. One for the advanced. A complicated combination of piaffe followed by a canter half-pirouette, rounded off by a tricky triple hop manoeuvre.

that enables one to flaunt one's savoir-faire and one's manly fecundity simultaneously. It is called 'Supermarket Dressage'.

Increasing numbers of fellows now regard the tawdry aisles of Waitrose or Sainsbury's as an ideal dressage arena. Based loosely on its classical equestrian counterpart, Supermarket Dressage consists of a rigid series of highly stylised manoeuvres designed to display a man's agility, aesthetic judgement and general road-worthiness to the gathered throng of fillies. Fidelity to classical dressage is much encouraged (where practical), although in the early days of the sport, attempts to smuggle Shetland ponies into branches of Tescos in lieu of proper dressage horses ended in disaster and nearly killed the practice in its infancy. Today the adoption of beautifully carved Victorian hobbyhorses is seen as the best way of introducing a charming note of authenticity to proceedings.

The routine commences at the sliding doors of the chosen emporium. A contestant starts his performance with a light half-canter into the fresh fruit and veg section, pausing only to retrieve one apple from those on display. He is then required to perform various tests (See figs. 1 & 2) including ser-

pentines, leg-yields, counter canters, canter half-pirouettes, trot zigzag half-passes and piaffes, taking in along the way a precise series of shop sections: including the cheese counter (where a pound of farmhouse Stilton is requested), the pastes and spreads section (where homage is given to the Gentleman's Relish) and the preserves (where the shelves are scoured for a jar of Old Thedgeley's 'Chunky Cut' Marmalade).

By this stage any young ladies who have found themselves moved by the performance will have gathered at the so-called 'check-out' in the hope of receiving from the beau that chooses them the ultimate accolade of the Cox's Pippin picked up at the beginning of the competition. (Any fellow who inadvertently presents a potential suitor with the tasteless flesh of a Golden Delicious, hurriedly picked up in error, is quite rightly regarded with universal contempt.)

After handing over the fruit, the couple leave arm in arm together with a small bag of comestible items to be consumed discreetly in more salubrious surroundings, Supermarket Dressage having catered to the requirements of love, style and gastronomy in one fell swoop.

AERONAUTICAL ELEGANCE

Torquil Arbuthnot and Nathaniel Slipper inspect today's airlines for their suitability in transporting civilised persons around the world

Most readers will doubtless own their own aeroplane, if not their own airline. However, shortened circumstances caused by the unexpectedly rough going at Ascot may lead to the temporary loss of one's Learjet or twin-prop. Consequently one is forced to travel with the commercial airlines. Certain bearded readers, those of Fabian persuasion, may wish to ape Mr Orwell in his *Down and Out in Paris and London* days and travel by Economy class, but the discerning Chap could do worse than follow these simple suggestions in order to travel in the elegant style to which one has become accustomed.

One should always embark on a voyage in high spirits; therefore it is essential to spend as little time as possible in the airport. Fondly remembered aerodromes full of spirited fellows and their flying machines made of brown paper, sticky tape and balsawood have been swept away by that infernal beast, progress. You may find yourself led to believe that before boarding an aeroplane, you will be able to do a little clothes shopping, browse through a collection of nineteenth-century French literature and Enid Blyton books for the flight, and then settle your stomach with a fine luncheon at one of the many stylish café-bars available. Sadly the truth is brutally different, and one may find oneself under the impression of being in a vision of hell that even Dante would have blushed to describe, the level of hell known as *familias vulgaris (cum childrus)* .

To avoid this Victorian freak show, it is necessary to send one's valet ahead to collect the billets, make financial arrangements to ensure that any unfortunate incidents in your past are overlooked at passport control and to reserve your seats in the upper circle and a large vodka and tonic for the interval. You then simply saunter onto the plane a few moments before take-off, raising your eyebrows deliciously at the stewardess as you pass. By now, your valet will have reported any incidents of note, and any passengers whom it might be efficacious to befriend or hide from on the journey to come.

Upon boarding the aircraft ask the steward to escort you to the promenade deck. Should he attempt vulgar familiarity and say something like, "You're in 23D, sir, straight down the aisle," belabour him with your Malacca until he remembers his place and bows and scrapes appropriately. Airline seats are notoriously uncomfortable so do remember to take on board your own leopardskin chaise longue or rattan lounger. Note that the No Smoking signs refer only to the more inferior brands of cigarettes and do not apply to your own Sobranies, Monte Cristos, hookah, Piccadilly Old Shag or Moroccan Woodbines.

Food on aeroplanes is tawdry fare, but do not be cowed by the officiousness of the chippies (or "stewardesses"): state firmly, "I will begin with quails' eggs stuffed with truffled caviar, followed by saddle of Sandringham venison with pommes Bernanos, and will finish with a simple Stilton sorbet. A Pouilly Fouisse; then two bottles of the Montrachet '65; a tawny port; and a glass or two of your admirable Madeira to finish." Fearing the worst, though, the aeronautical chap will ensure

that his valet has a Fortnum & Mason hamper upon his person.

Do not leave your baggage out of your sight, as it will surely be pilfered by the avaricious riff-raff travelling steerage. Have your man load the guncases, japanned trunks, Vuitton travel-o-bar, etc, in the back of the aircraft, and have him stand guard over it with his trusty Webley. The revolver is necessary since air-piracy (or "hijacking") is all too common these days. A chap should always arm himself with a brace of revolvers and a Malay *kris* to repel air-pirates. Sadly, one can no longer rely on the regimented muscles of the SAS to rescue one

from these ruffians, since most of their "squaddies" are too busy writing penny-shocker novelettes to bother with the tedium of soldiery.

The "in-flight entertainment" will doubtless be a kinematic film entitled *Ninja Kickboxer 3*. Do your fellow passengers a courtesy by disabling the kine-projector and inaugurating some amusing party games such as Dumb Crambo, Hunt the Bengal Tiger and Musical Chairs.

After a satisfactory luncheon and a light *bhang*-induced doze, it is high time to pay a visit to the cockpit to introduce yourself to the captain. Do not be disappointed when you discover that airline pilots these days are little more than glorified bus-conductors, since all the actual flying is now done by a modern electronic computing apparatus.

Indeed, upon entering the cockpit you will find the captain and a large dog. The captain is there to feed the dog and the dog is there to bite the captain should he attempt to touch any of the controls. Once your valet has subdued the dog, the captain will be only too delighted to allow you to fly the aeroplane. With a jolly cry of, "Let's see what the old bus can do," show the admiring captain how you won the DFC in 1944, avoiding the flak bat-teries over Berlin by flying underneath the Glienicke Bridge with three ME109s on your tail.

NB: Incidentally, if any aspiring birdman wishes to learn how to fly, they are advised not bother with flying lessons and the like. One can pick up all one needs merely from reading the works of literary aeronauts such as Saint-Exupéry, and d'Annunzio.

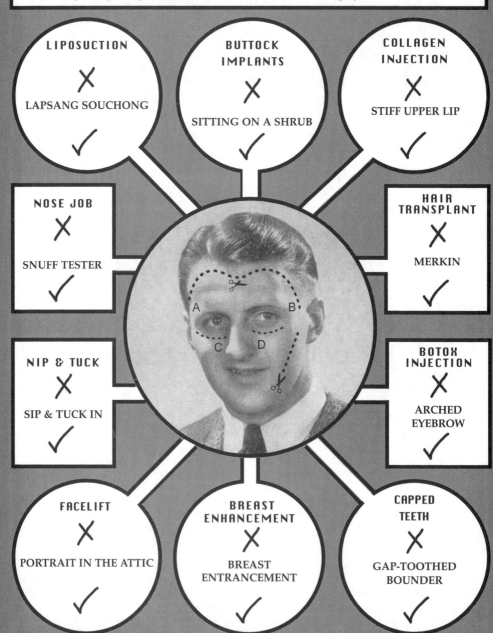

COSMETIC PURGATORY. We consulted that dipsomaniac apothecary and disgraced plastic surgeon, Sir Roderick "Chopping board" Picklesworth, on the gentlemanly approach to bodily improvements. He kindly interrupted an interesting experiment in bowler hat grafting to explain the Dos and Don'ts of cosmetic surgery.

LIPOSUCTION
✗
LAPSANG SOUCHONG
✓

BUTTOCK IMPLANTS
✗
SITTING ON A SHRUB
✓

COLLAGEN INJECTION
✗
STIFF UPPER LIP
✓

NOSE JOB
✗
SNUFF TESTER
✓

HAIR TRANSPLANT
✗
MERKIN
✓

NIP & TUCK
✗
SIP & TUCK IN
✓

BOTOX INJECTION
✗
ARCHED EYEBROW
✓

FACELIFT
✗
PORTRAIT IN THE ATTIC
✓

BREAST ENHANCEMENT
✗
BREAST ENTRANCEMENT
✓

CAPPED TEETH
✗
GAP-TOOTHED BOUNDER
✓

A   B
C   D

GENTLE MANLY REQUISITES

CIGAR CUTTERS

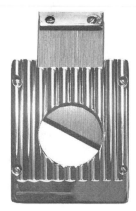

Is an unclipped tip giving you gyp? Has your chopper come a cropper? Is your Corona making you a moaner? Do you suffer from debilitating conditions such as 'suction deficit disorder' or 'clag teat'? Well, wave goodbye to fumatory frustration and positively sprint down to your local tobacconist in search of some quality cigar cutters. Almost as if designed by a Lilliputian Monsieur Guillotine, cigar cutters are guaranteed to munch their way through the heftiest of Havanas, and can effectively double up as a handy chopping implement for asparagus, baby corn or the fingers of particularly recalcitrant children.

"By jingo, Sir, now you look as if your Havana really good time."

CIGAR CUTTERS
Available from :
G. Smith and Sons,
74 Charing Cross Road,
London WC2H 0BG
@ £8.95

Howard Spent investigates

THE SEMIOTICS OF EYEWEAR

S ome time ago, a reader of this august periodical wrote to suggest that I turned my semiotic observations towards the realm of eyewear. The reader (whose name I am sadly unable to recall) rather flippantly suggested that the title could be Semioptics. Though such blatant tomfoolery would be enough to alienate most serious men of science, I pride myself on never dismissing the musings of the layman merely because they may initially appear ill-hewn or irritatingly jocular. Indeed it will no doubt strike seasoned readers of this section that the appraisal of a man's human condition, social status and psychological profile merely through the optical instruments he chooses to secure to his face is an eminently reasonable avenue of semiological enquiry.

The eyes, if we are to believe popular sentiment, are the windows to the soul and act as dual conduits by which we perceive and are perceived by the outside world. Our language is peppered with phrases relating to our eyes. Gents often see eye to eye or endeavour to browbeat one another, and as far as the ladies are concerned making eyes, winking or maintaining a mischievous glint are all essential weapons in the art of wooing. It is beyond the scope of this article (and indeed this publication) to venture too deeply into the abstruse (and often disturbing) ways of womanhood, but it might be noted in passing that ladies are far more adept at realising the full potential of their ocular orbs than we are. The eyes to the average female are what the sting is to the scorpion – a formidable weapon, ever poised and pregnant with deadly allure. Much time and

effort is taken to attract attention to them through the use of gaudy pigment and false eyelashes. It is telling indeed that Saint Lucy became so aware of the attracting power of her own dainty orbs that she was prepared to tear them out, rather than subject herself to the ravishings of a potential suitor.

But, dear reader, I find myself teetering on the edge of digression into an area better left to a future article. For the moment, let us return to the gentleman and the way in which he chooses to frame or otherwise enhance his visual apparatus. All fellows at one time or another have found it useful or necessary to adopt optical equipment to improve their eyesight or appearance. From the jeweller's eyeglass to the many species of spectacle; from Innuit snow goggles to monocles, whatever contraption a chap elects to wear it is bound to speak volumes about his state of mind, his future hopes and his stolen dreams. If the eyes are the windows to the soul, then a pair of spectacles or other ocular adherence may act as the gailypainted shutters, the elaborate pediments, the ornate stucco work, or, indeed, the veritable window-boxes of a man's psyche.

So keep a sharp eye out for the varieties illustrated in the following pages. A keen observation of one's fellow man in the realm of opthalmological enhancement will provide you with a head start in the game of life, and will allow you instantaneously to judge the difference between decent fellow and utter scoundrel. The semiotics of eyewear is guaranteed to prove an invaluable aid for use socially, in business and for pleasure.

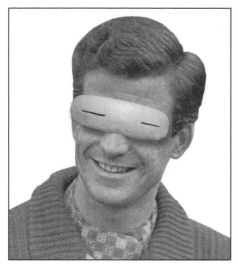

The Pretentious

Hand-crafted Innuit snow goggles are apparently à-la-mode with the indigenous peoples of Alaska, but such eyewear is infra dig. when donned as 'ethno-fashion' by those who inexplicably decide to dwell in the inhospitable wastes of Notting Hill.

The Theatrical

The 15th Earl of Camardenshire's family are willing to turn a blind eye to his 'artistic' tastes in clothing, but are dismayed that his choice of spectacles demote him from the haughty echelons of genuine peerage to the lowly role of pantomime dame.

The Louche

Regarded by some as the apogee of ocular apparatus, the lorgnette is a perfect choice for the exquisite or decadent gentleman. It is particularly suited for lascivious ogling as bedouin boyservants gyrate shamelessly to the intoxicating rhythms of Beelzebub.

The Post-Ironic

By self-consciously donning a pair of 'nerdy' glasses and replicating the fashion errors of his forefathers this fellow believes that he is being 'with it' and knowing. Slavish adherence to the dictates of fashion is a degenerate's method of bolstering flagging self-esteem.

The Prosthetic

A chap of bravado and spunk won't allow a simple war wound to diminish his usefulness. The possession of a glass eye is something that all young turks can aspire to. It is particularly efficacious in keeping children entertained at parties or whilst babysitting.

The Adenoidal

Pince-nez are secured to the face by the touchingly literal Gallic expedient of 'pinching the nose'. This optical item has long been associated with the excesses of the avant-garde intelligentsia, which no doubt accounts for the particularly nasal tones of the French tongue.

The Sublime

The universal badge of seniority and savoir-faire, the monocle is the hallmark of the man to be reckoned with. Its effectiveness is somewhat diminished, however, if sported in conjunction with well-meaning but crudely-crafted items knitted by one's maiden aunt.

The Vulgar

Common-or-garden rock stars or has-been disc jockeys sometimes imagine that the wearing of sunglasses is enough to render them masculine, sexually potent and youthful. Concealing the direction of one's gaze is the first refuge of a scoundrel.

The Studious

This pitiful acned boffin would rather strap a jeweller's glass to his eye and ponder the mating habits of ants than seek the love of a robust young lady of child-bearing age. The rarefied world of academe is all too often a disguise for sexual inadequacy.

The Ridiculous

Moral bankruptcy and a dearth of imagination can lead to a fellow trying to win favour by wearing novelty sunglasses of outlandish proportions. This nincompoop fondly imagines himself to be rather eccentric and 'off the wall'. He most definitely is not.

The Calculating

This stylish cove is acutely aware of the importance of being correctly equipped for a night at the theatre. Opera glasses are an essential viewing device for 'casing' the priceless baubles laying atop the perfectly framed contents of a burgeoning décolletage.

The Vain

A fellow can find himself so intoxicated by his own physical beauty that he is unwilling to pollute his features with spectacles. This deluded specimen might be better advised to jettison his contact lenses altogether lest he stray too close to a mirror.

THE CHAP
ROOM

Sheridan Coxcombe examines the intricate mysteries of the Internet

THERE IS A QUESTION THAT MANY OF US ARE ASKING ourselves these days, and it is this: "What is the Internet and can it be of any use to a gentleman?" The answer generally perceived to be the most accurate is: "Leave the beastly thing alone and your pleasant life of indolence will not be affected in the slightest." However, if curiosity does get the better of you, it is important that you are aware of the true potential of the Internet.

The Internet has the potential to frustrate, enrage, irritate and generally corrupt the very soul of any gent worth his salt. Should you find yourself powerless to resist the mild inquisitiveness provoked by all the hooh-hah surrounding this new-fangled device, I would like to offer a few sage words, if I may, of guidance.

The Internet is an extremely complicated contraption which, even when its functions are explained by a competent person, still manages to remain entirely incomprehensible. Conversations on all matters relating to the Internet are apt to produce an intense throbbing about the temples, coupled with an overwhelming desire to throw oneself out of a window.

The only practical method for a gentleman to get his Martini-soaked noddle around the concept of the Internet is to try and make a comparison between the infernal piece of mechanical wizardry and his own oak-panelled study. Let us navigate our way through some of the terminology as if we were ambling our way into an afternoon steeped in the world of belles lettres within the cosy confines of our study.

LOGGING ON

What the technophiles call 'logging on to the Internet' can be compared to opening the door to one's study. Once 'on-line' (or seated comfortably at your enormous leather-covered mahogany desk) you will need to engage the services of a 'search engine'. This is the technological (and therefore rather prosaic) equivalent of your eager Moroccan houseboy, whom you are often in the habit of commanding to fetch you a slim volume of verse from the upper shelves of your towering personal library. The ladder which the little fellow willingly scampers up is referred to in Internet-speak as your 'browser'.

When he brings the requested tome to your desk and you begin leafing through it in search of a choice quotation, this process is what the technophiles call 'searching a website'. To simulate the 'searching' experience with more authenticity, try dropping the book on the floor every now and again, or suddenly, just as you think you are about to find the quotation you seek, snapping the book shut and losing your place. An even more dramatic note of authenticity can be added by tipping yourself back on your chair, falling to the floor, knocking yourself out, and regaining consciousness with a splitting headache and bleary eyes.

ELECTRONIC MESSAGES

Now that you have observed some websites, you are ready to send an email. The term 'email' is an abbreviation of 'esoteric mailing system'. The process works like this: you type a message; the message is whizzed up to a magical centre somewhere in the cosmos, and then it is bounced down to the recipient through some diabolick process. The nearest approximation in your study to this process is the following: Insert a fresh sheet of Basildon Bond into your Remington typewriter; without bothering to use the capitalization or punctuation keys, bash out a brief message, abbreviating random words and making sure that your spelling is appalling. For example:

my deer peregrine
wd luv to c u later this wknd. How about poping over one evng for a spot of pimms and a game of cribij
   yours
   sheridan

Rip the completed message out of the typewriter, hand it to your footman and ask him to deliver it to the address you give him. Give him a few hundred pounds in cash as well, in case the recipient lives abroad and he has to catch an aeroplane to reach him. In such cases, request that your footman waits to be given a reply before returning to England.

WEBCAMS

There are some highly diverting websites available that feature what are known as 'live web cams'. This is techno-speak for 'live kinetic transmission apparatus'. The best comparison for these is the powerful telescope you keep at the window of your study trained on the bathroom window of the house across the road from you. When you observe the charming young lady who lives there performing her ablutions, what you are doing is the equivalent of 'logging on' to the 'live web cam' of her 'home page'. Complete this illusion by shaking the telescope violently, occasionally clapping your hand over the lens, and hurling a

wad of ten-pound notes into the wastepaper basket every time you see anything interesting.

AN EXERCISE

To really simulate the full joys of the Internet in your study, try the following exercise. Come into your study at 9 am with the express intention of checking the birth date of Lord Byron. Spend the whole morning rifling through hundreds of your books, keeping Youssef running up and down the stepladder until he's panting with exhaustion. Get sidetracked from your task by suddenly running over to the telescope, spending a fruitless 45 minutes trying to train it on the right room in the house

opposite, only to observe the charming young lady's grandfather busy on the lavatory. Get back to your searches for Lord Byron's birth date, then suddenly rush out to a travel agent and book two tickets to Tunisia with no particular reduction in cost. After eight hours, leave the study in a state of nervous exhaustion, having completely forgotten why you wanted to know Lord Byron's birth date in the first place.

And there in a nutshell, gentlemen, you have a precise simulacrum of the joys of the Internet. Take my advice and leave the bally thing alone.

A YEAR IN CATFORD

Provençal *vignerons* DIDIER and VERONIQUE CAUDILLON did what their Aix neighbours had only ever dreamed of – buying an authentic South London council flat and living in *Le Style Anglais* for a year. This is the first instalment of their diary for that unforgettable year in Catford, London SE6.

The 2002 Gault-Millau guide describes the Catford franchise of Dixy Fried Chicken as 'the nearest the French traveller is likely to get to the authentic *Catfordois* dining experience'. A posse of teenage girls enjoying a post prandial cigarette in the entrance, their pale *embonpoints* sagging out of nylon tracksuits, was testament to the restaurant's popularity with the locals.

We passed below the neo-modernist *façade* composed of large slabs of brightly coloured Perspex with a comical tricolore chicken motif (though the colour scheme referred to America's finger-lickin' deep south), to be greeted by the maître d'. This was a middle-aged gentleman from the Levant, whose moustache, sleek with airborne lipids, quivered with puzzlement when we announced that we had reserved a table for two. We wondered whether, like Maison Lefevre in our Provençal home, Dixy operates on a first come, first served basis. Like all the best restaurants, Dixy has few tables – in fact there is only one, which was occupied by a rugged old *clochard* of Scottish descent enjoying a tin of the local moonshine. After a spot of good-natured badinage with the maître d', he surrendered his table to us.

When we asked to view the menu, the maître d' merely raised his eyes heavenwards, and above his head we saw a charming fluorescent display of the day's fare, accompanied by helpful colour illustrations. We have always adopted a 'when in Rome' policy on our gastronomic voyages, so we asked the maître d' what the *plat du jour* was. He motioned a bandaged thumb towards an illustration bearing the enticing sobriquet of 'Family bucket chicken nugget mega meal'.

Within a few seconds, a pimpled youth put his head over the counter and said, "D'you want coke or Fanta with that, mate?"

"*Attendez, monsieur,*" we said, consulting our Gault-Millau for guidance. We read that it is an English custom to serve a complimentary beverage with meals such as these, so we grasped the opportunity of sampling the local tipple and plumped for the coca-cola. The food was superb: breaded *brochettes* of reconstituted *poule* with *porc* traces drizzled with *sauce tomate*, with deep-fried shards of potato-flavoured monosodium glutamate, accompanied by *juliennes* of cabbage, carrot and onion in a sweetened *aioli*, all served in a rustic cardboard bucket.

As our first English luncheon battled its way into our digestive systems, we realised what an adventure it was going to be adapting ourselves to South London gastronomic customs over the coming year.

Like so many Provençals, we had often returned from our customary annual *sojourn* in London with the feeling of having only scraped the surface of that wonderful city. It was like being wrenched away from an urban paradise, making our life on a 34-acre farm in the Luberon Mountains seem humdrum and monotonous. Our modest vineyard, our

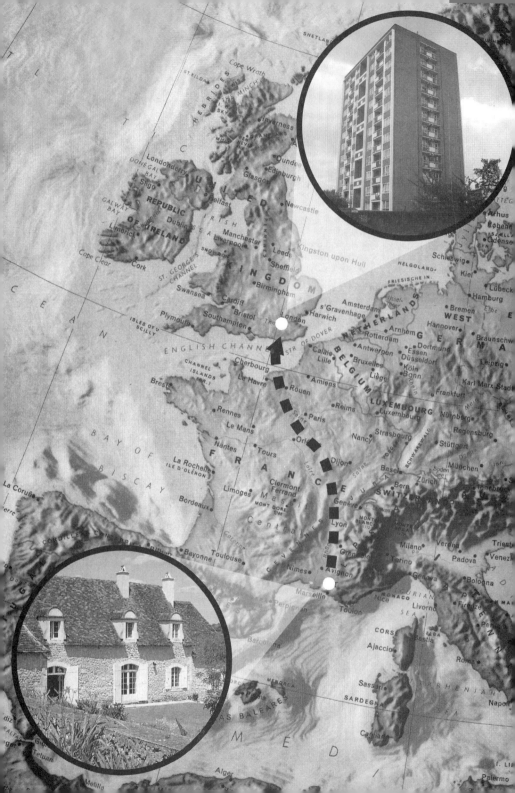

three goats, our olive oil press, our swimming pool with views over the mountains, lunches with neighbours that lasted all afternoon under cloudless azure skies – they were all very well, but we often yearned for a life more steeped in the edgy, gritty urban authenticity that can only be found across the Channel. So one year we thought we'd make a go of it. Rent out our six-bedroom farmhouse in Provence to some gullible Britons, take a little maisonette in Catford and see what Providence threw at us.

The estate agents we contacted in Catford seemed more than eager to help us find a 'typical' abode in the area, and after viewing several *chi-chi* apartments in nearby Blackheath, we soon found exactly what we were looking for: a dilapidated ex-local authority two-bedroom flat on the Dregnor Estate, between Catford Shopping Centre and the Catford Gun Company.

The flat needed a few repairs, for the previous tenants seemed to have left in rather a hurry. There were curious scorch marks up the walls, the doors had large holes in them, and the floor was a carpet of empty beer cans and hypodermic syringes. The fixtures and fittings had all been removed, so effectively we would be buying a blank canvas to decorate as we wished. *"C'est vraiment charmant!"* we shouted to the estate agent, knocking on his locked car window. £250,000 and a surprisingly small amount of paperwork later, number 23, Dregnor House, Catford was ours.

Since our vision was to abandon our simple Provençal ways and immerse ourselves in the authentic British Metropolitan existence, we wanted to decorate the flat entirely in *Le Style Anglais*. We would spend a year eating, drinking and sleeping exactly as the Catfordians did, and after a year, *qui sait?* We might even settle here for good.

The first step was to have the water, gas, electricity and telephone reconnected. We were asked to supply monumental amounts of identification, birth certificates, blood tests etc, before any negotiations took place. The previous tenants must have been a lively lot! Life at Dregnor House must have been one long party – and we were determined to keep things on a similarly crazy footing!

We purchased a large fridge, several cases of lager, a CD player and some discs by local musicians. Matching nylon tracksuits completed the picture, and we spent the first evening of our new life in a whirl of Tennents Super, Pringles (wafer-thin slices of pan-fried starch marinated in essence of shallot and *fromage*) and the evocative strains of 'So Solid Crew'. The neighbours, drawn to the sounds of music and good cheer emanating from our flat, were eager to introduce themselves, and soon the flat was a medley of friendly faces. In the

spirit of good neighbourliness, we kept up a steady supply of lager to our new friends, trotting up and down the seven flights of stairs to the off licence that never seemed to close.

In the ambience of cordiality, one of our neighbours must have mistaken our stereo for his own, as it was missing by the morning. But here was the joy of council flat dwelling: we would only have to put the word out, and we felt sure that the mistake would soon be rectified.

We soon realized that social life in our block tended to revolve around the sound system. Our neighbours rather quaintly tried to outdo each other throughout the day by cranking up the dials on the stereo equipment. We lived among the perpetual rattle and boom of competing sound systems, leading to constant headaches and small piles of brick dust in the corner of the living room. We loved it. This was *La Vie de Riley*.

It was clear that the essential requisite for an authentic Catfordian lifestyle – the SE6 equivalent of our four-metre stone outdoor dining table in Provence – was a state-of-the-art sound system. But how would we find *la chose authentique*? We consulted advertisements in shop windows and local newspapers placed by disc jockeys on their uppers. After making a few calls, we found ourselves in the tiny bedroom of a fellow who called himself MC 50-pence for a living – although his parents had addressed him as Otis when ushering us into his boudoir.

Otis/50-pence had an impressive array of machinery, which the constraints of an impoverished background and being fifteen had not appeared to hinder. We returned to our flat with over £3,000-worth of audio equipment and 50-pence's assurance that it would produce some 'mongin' sounds.

For the remainder of our home décor, we set off on Sunday morning to one of South East London's famous markets. Sedgehill Field Boot Sale takes place every week from 6 am in a muddy field off Southend Lane. The boot sale is as much a social occasion as an opportunity to trade household items. A powerful smell fills the air, a blend of strong tea, fried onions, cigarettes and last night's booze. Couples manning the stalls mainly consisted of a rotund lady swaddled in pink velour, sucking on a Raffles king size and putting on a brave face, while her hungover-looking husband lurked near his car reeking of old pub and probably wishing he were dead. We breakfasted in *Le Style*

Catfordois – tranches of *porc fumé* in a griddled *brioche* drizzled with *sauce brune*.

Searching in vain for the type of stall you find in Provençal markets, piled high with pungent cheeses, fresh fruit and tasty viands, the nearest we found was one old costermonger selling family packs of Wagon Wheels. Most of the stalls specialized in second-hand clothes, toys and bric-a-brac, some peddling indispensable requisites such as novelty lighters, large smoking papers and Duracell batteries.

This was an opportunity of decorating the flat with genuine Catfordian cast-offs. We ended up with a marvellous collection of souvenir plates from Mallorca, some plastic-framed prints of puppies and kittens, a couple of copper reliefs depicting village scenes and some horse brasses. When it came to clothes we were spoilt for choice. There were tracksuits – *de rigueur* among the Catfordian populace – in every size, shape, colour and style, whose brand names were all very similar: Tommy Hillfiger, Tony Halfrigger and Timmy Hellfinger.

By the time we had left the market, the hour was inching its way towards one o'clock, which could only mean one thing.

This particular Sunday we were in the mood to sample the delights of the famous English 'pub lunch'. A number of local places were recommended by the Gault-Millau, but as we drove in search of one we passed a tavern that seemed to epitomize the traditional English pub. Its name was The Green Man. We tossed our Gault-Millau into the back seat of the car and entered its doors.

The saloon style interior was instantly appealing. At several of the tables sat clusters of wounded young soccer *aficionados* nursing the previous day's scars with Stella Artois, sucking on Benson & Hedges for added comfort. At the bar, their middle-aged counterparts (their parents?) swaggered about displaying their enormous *embonpoints* and their sunburned tattoos, engaging in playful badinage richly peppered with their coarse *argot*.

We took a table and ordered a round of chilled lagers to whet our appetites for a stupendous Sunday feast. Much like Les Deux Garçons in Aix, The Green Man has no menu. At Les Deux Garçons this is because the day's delicious fare is the spontaneous creation of the eccentric 3-Michelin-starred chef, Laurent Desoux. At Catford's The Green Man, the reason there is no menu is because there is no food. Our requests for the bill of fare were greeted with much hilarity by the fellows ensconced at the bar. So we asked them

to suggest to us what the typical Catfordian would do for his Sunday luncheon.

"Stick around mate, we'll show you."

This seemed like a good opportunity to discover the local customs at first hand, so at their invitation, we joined the hearty fellows for a lager or two more. As the guests, we felt that etiquette demanded that we pay for the drinks, and soon the jovial gathering had swollen to fifteen or twenty locals.

There is a not unpleasant (though not wholly pleasant) numbing around the temples that is the result of several flagons of draught lager. With persistent consumption, a further sensation begins to occur which can best be compared to having one's eyeballs removed, allowing someone to play table tennis with them, then wrapping them in sandpaper and replacing them in the skull. By 8 pm, with only a packet of salt and vinegar crisps under our belts, we asked our new friends when the aforementioned 'bite to eat' would take place. "Don't worry about that mate. Mine's a pint of Fosters and a double Southern Comfort."

At half past ten we finally emerged, swaying from The Green Man into the chill night air. Our friend led us towards what they promised would "make you wish you'd drank a few more lagers!"

We sincerely doubted it, as they bundled us into an establishment named 'Best Turkish Kebab'. The smell within was too overpowering for us, so we waited outside.

Presently our friends emerged carrying armfuls of paper packages, two of which they handed to us. We copied our acquaintances by tucking into them right there in the street, under a light drizzle, our faces lit by the glare of neon and passing car headlights. The repast turned out to be the most delicious meal we had ever tasted. A *pain levain* filled with slices of a spit-fired lamb-flavoured offal *terrine*, which we could see blistering in the window of the establishment, with a *julienne* of *salade tiede* and a unique chili *jus*. Every mouthful seemed to fill some aching chasm created by the volumes of lager inside us.

Although we were used to long lingering lunches of seven or eight courses, accompanied by several different wines and punctuated by a *trou Normand* – a light serving of sorbet to cleanse the palate between courses – the English tradition had its own peculiar charm. The afternoon had been one long *trou Catfordois* between a long-forgotten breakfast and this Middle Eastern midnight repast.

At a grand total of £164.76, including an afternoon's worth of lager, a large doner kebab for each of our hosts and several packets of Benson & Hedges, lunch *a-la-Catford* had not come cheap, but it had certainly been an authentic English experience.

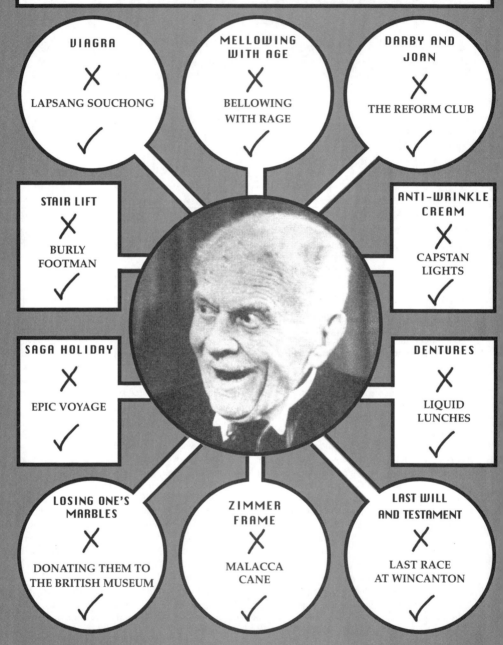

VIAGRA
✗
LAPSANG SOUCHONG
✓

MELLOWING WITH AGE
✗
BELLOWING WITH RAGE
✓

DARBY AND JOAN
✗
THE REFORM CLUB
✓

STAIR LIFT
✗
BURLY FOOTMAN
✓

ANTI-WRINKLE CREAM
✗
CAPSTAN LIGHTS
✓

SAGA HOLIDAY
✗
EPIC VOYAGE
✓

DENTURES
✗
LIQUID LUNCHES
✓

LOSING ONE'S MARBLES
✗
DONATING THEM TO THE BRITISH MUSEUM
✓

ZIMMER FRAME
✗
MALACCA CANE
✓

LAST WILL AND TESTAMENT
✗
LAST RACE AT WINCANTON
✓

CLASSIFIED ADS

SITUATIONS VACANT

Picturesque hermit, with at least 3 years' experience, required. An exciting opportunity to work with the landscape gardening team at Floodsbury House, Wiltshire. Must be in possession of long white beard and able (when tracked down) to entertain visitors with rare nuggets of bucolic insight. Preference will be given to the candidate who can demonstrate an ability to survive on a diet of woodland fungi, frog spawn and small rodents. Dank cave supplied. No vegetarians. Telephone Floodsbury 045

Houseboy required for large rambling mansion in Wigan. Duties to include basic errands, housework, parlour games and Mexican wrestling. Would suit almond-eyed Turk of no fixed abode. Accommodation and weekly rations of Vermouth, Gentleman's Relish and body lotion provided. Call Wigan 249.

Assassin. Disinherited peer, inexperienced in such matters, requires the services of a professional hitman to 'cash in the chips' of close family member. Five-figure payment as soon as title and deeds to extensive estates have been transferred to own name. Confidentiality guaranteed. Contact: Julian, 12th Viscount of Tiverton (pending), on Tarvin 905

PET SERVICES

AVUNC-U-LIKE uncle walking service for tired, lonely or depressed uncles. Our walkers are fully trained in pipe filling, Times Crossword assistance and leather elbow-patch maintenance. Uncles are walked in groups of maximum six in local parkland, with a visit to a pub. Their tweeds get an airing, they get to meet other uncles, and they are given a listening ear to their half-baked theories on space travel and bovine telepathy. Call Preston 064.

Panther Hire. Make an impression the next time you visit the opera or a film premiere. Hire one of our range of big cats as the ultimate fashion accessory. Diamond studded collars and insurance on request. Phone Stroud 499

CHILDREN'S ENTERTAINERS

"MR BEAST" – unique magic act for children's parties, featuring Black Mass, devil-worship, hobgoblin invoking and sinister chanting. Kids will love this dark night of the soul; guaranteed emotional instability for a lifetime. Call Hounslow 666.

"MAD" MALCOLM THE CLOWN, for birthdays, christenings, circumcisions. "Mad" Malcolm is a clown with a difference – he isn't funny! Look, kiddies, who's that lurking in the garden with too much mascara and a ginger wig, sharing a bottle of Teachers and a packet of woodbines with little Simon – it's "Mad" Malcolm! Contact Malcolm at Secure Unit, HMP Belmarsh.

HOUSEHOLD SERVICES

MR BEAU CRUMPLE. Break in newly tailored suits, trousers and jackets the easy way. Our staff of fully-qualified suit trainers can give your pristine attire that 'lived in/died in' look much favoured by the English aristocracy. We employ only tried-and-tested techniques such as thrashing about on heather moorland or sleeping in gutters. Satisfaction guaranteed. Scarborough 277

EXOTIC SHEDS. Tired of pottering about in your shabby, dilapidated garden shed? Let us convert it into a Turkish bath, an Indian marble pleasure palace or even a fully staffed Moroccan Souk with a realistic desert surround! If you've recently had a few complaints from your neighbours about the height of your hedge – give them something to really witter about! Call Stockport 351.

GENTLE MANLY REQUISITES

THE SPATTERDASH

Does dampness in your ankles make you rankle? Is abrasive heather scuffing your shiny shoe leather? Are chilly winds giving you aches in your pins? Well fret no more, it is about time you sought out the advice of Maria Carey about her exciting new range of spats (short for spatterdash) specifically designed for the rigours of the 21st century. Laugh in the face of puddles and keep your fetlocks free from draughts in the most stylish way known to mankind. Maria's spats are reassuringly constructed from a range of high quality materials. Illustrated is a waxed cotton spat for robust urban useage.

"Maria Carey maketh the spats and the spats maketh the man."

GLOBAL CHAPITALISM

Chappish dispatches from foreign parts and other places on the outer edges of civilization

MONOFOCALLY CHALLENGED

That local newspaper for the Home Counties, the *Daily Mail*, recently featured a touching article by Sir Patrick Moore lamenting the demise of the monocle. It seems that Britain's last manufacturer of the single eyeglass, Dolland and Aitchison, has ceased production of monocles due to lack of demand. Sir Patrick informs his readers that fortunately he has enough monocle frames to last him a lifetime, since the lenses themselves can be replaced by any competent optician. The cosmos-scrutinizing knight of the realm has worn a monocle since he was 16 years old, when an optician told him that he needed a minor right-eye enhancement, while his left eye required no ophthalmic intervention.

Since launching himself as perhaps the only teenager ever to sport such singular eye-wear, Sir Patrick has never looked back, and now claims to feel undressed without his monocle. *The Chap* peers at him mono-focally and nods heartily in agreement.

TENTATIVE TENTACLES

It has come to *The Chap*'s attention that the male octopus has a most gentlemanly manner of making love to the ladies. Rather than engage in any fumbled three-second unpleasantness like many other animals, the octopus inseminates his mate through the deployment of a simple hand gesture. It works like this: a lady octopus observes the body postures and skin patterns of the various male octopuses vying for her attention. When she has selected a suitably postured and decorated mate, she sits back and waits for the mating process to begin. Mr Octopus gingerly approaches Mrs Octopus and lurks a few feet away from her, blobbing about in his charming octopussian way. He then stretches out his third right arm, which is hectocotylized with sperm sacs, as languidly as possible, and deposits spermatophores into Mrs Octopus's mantle cavity.

And that's it. Mrs Octopus then retreats under a rock to incubate her eggs, and Mr Octopus goes about his business. How utterly civilized! *The Chap* extends a languid tentacle to the octopus, and hopes that his mating tactics will be imitated in some of the seedy discotheques where humans blob about on a Saturday night.

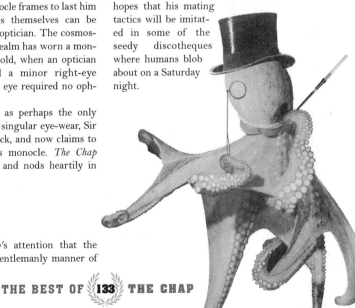

Howard Spent investigates

THE SEMIOTICS OF NECKWEAR

Symbolically the neck is a highly significant area of a fellow's anatomy, forming as it does a vital isthmus between his cerebral functions (the head) and the means by which he converts his desires into action (the body). Naturally, most chaps aren't much concerned with the 'action' side of things, usually being content to dwell in the arena of the mind whilst lounging for endless hours on a divan, consuming volumes of decadent poetry, pungent hasheesh by the bucketload and hardly stirring a muscle. But when a man is unexpectedly deprived of connection with his body either by summary execution, paralysis or by over indulgence in Emerald Scimitars (a mind-boggling cocktail constructed of 4 parts absinthe, 7 parts raki and 1 part creosote) he begins to realise what he takes for granted. Even the modicum of energy required to turn the page of a book, lift the nozzle of one's hookah to one's lips or toddle of to the kitchen in pursuit of an olive or two, once denied us, would soon make us realise that a gent's psyche, perfumed and beautiful though it may be, still requires some input from the outside world to achieve its aims.

With this in mind it is not surprising that throughout history man has chosen to adorn this crucial and vulnerable part of his physique with various ornaments. Modern man often uses his neck to display his badges of office (from mayoral chain to priest's dog collar) or his sense of belonging (from club tie to masonic talisman), but even when a fellow finds himself at odds with such worldly ostentation, he still unconsciously projects to all and sundry whole volumes of information about himself merely by what he chooses to drape around or adhere to his wind pipe.

Dear Reader, I have spent the last three months observing how my fellow man betrays his inner life through laryngeal decoration. I have skulked awkwardly in changing rooms across the land, I have eyed people up in parties and parks (sometimes with unexpectedly alarming results), I have prodded and probed my way through the wardrobes of the rich and famous and I have consulted tailors, dandies, misfits, hooligans, working men and bank managers to gain their particular insights into the matter. Finally I have used my semiological nous to convert my observations into a cogent theory that may provide the reader with something very close to 'the truth'.

Over the next few pages I humbly submit a summary of my findings to you. I am sure you will find that they will prove an invaluable guide for use socially, in business, and for pleasure.

The Louche

With a polka-dot cravat, a stable of Moroccan house-boys and a soul mortgaged to the Prince of Darkness, this fellow singles himself out as the pinnacle of style. The mere ash from his cigarette should be scooped up and preserved as a sacred relic.

The Splendid

Despite its association with pompous academe, the bow tie is surely the loftiest achievement in the history of throat ornamentation. Emblematic of high mindedness and spiritual beauty, it should rightly be regarded as the silken-bladed propellor of the Infinite.

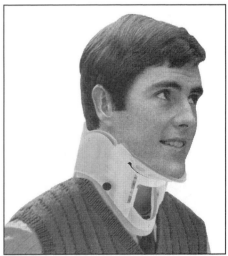

The Impotent

This burly young fellow may seem at first sight to epitomise the ideal standards of masculine beauty, but the withered paucity of his tie knot tells an entirely different tale. Parsimony in the neck region all too often heralds disappointment in the cantilever department.

The Licentious

The wearing of a neck brace is often assumed to be the unfortunate consequence of a foolhardy indulgence in the realm of sport, but it is just as likely to be the result of craning one's neck to catch a glimpse of a scantily clad neighbour performing her toilet.

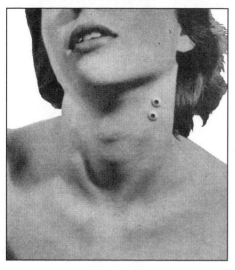

The Gothic

The 15th Earl's family are now resigned to his cross-dressing propensities, but by inflicting twin puncture marks on his neck and playing the ravished virgin, he is reducing the nobility of the House of Camarden to the gothic camp of Hammer House of Horror.

The Exotic

The growing hobby of auto-eroticism has made the noose this season's must-have fashion accessory. An idle fellow with time on his hands can have much fun with satsuma and amyl nitrate before having to return to the Commons in time for the Division Bell.

The Rustic

Worn by an artistic fop within the confines of his atelier, the neckerchief has certain bohemian credentials, but its association with campfires, folk music and other gin gang goolyism makes it an item that should be approached with extreme caution.

The Robust

Hirsute and happy he may be, but the chunky-knit excesses of Scandinavian fishermen and assorted ecological types are best avoided by the gentleman. The polo neck is only truly acceptable when worn for ill prepared and heroically fatal expeditions to the Antarctic.

The Dangerous

This vicious young hoodlum demonstrates his contempt for right-thinking modes of civilised behaviour by wearing a dog's collar in lieu of a dainty cravat. He'd better watch out, as such behaviour may well jeopardise his entry into the school philately society.

The Arriviste

A man ill at ease with new-found wealth may seek to display his fortune by wearing ostentatious jewellery of vulgar design. A true gentleman would only consider using gold for the fashioning of signet rings, cufflinks or exquisitely crafted shrines to Priapus.

The Classic

With over 85 ways of knotting a tie, a chap in a hurry may find himself indecisive as to which configuration to choose. If in doubt, the trusty Windsor will always hold one in good stead as an invisible shield against the unbridled rudery of the urban thoroughfare.

The Devil-May-Care

The ladies love a fellow who is unafraid to stand out from the crowd and entertain them with amusing tricks. This young fellow has turned a medical condition to his advantage by using his tracheotomy tube as an impromptu smoke ring blowing device.

ALUMNUS ELEGANTIS

Torquil Arbuthnot and *Nathaniel Slipper* *advise the university student on ways to ensure that his seat of learning is a sedan chair of opulence and debauchery*

Whilst this magazine offers much advice and counsel to those people to whom Chappism does not come naturally, it is vital that attention is paid to the next generation of gentlemen. Callow-faced youths may be too easily distracted from the path of dignity and sophistication by the barbaric caterwauls of popular music, or worse, the lure of denim and nylon. They may never know of the joy of the briar, the sparkle of a vodka martini or the pleasure of relieving Mr Ladbroke of 60 guineas after the 3.15 at Doncaster. The young are at their most vulnerable on fleeing the security of the family home or the public school, and being surrounded by like-minded ingrates who may have the audacity to assume that seventeen pints of "snakebite" in a sticky-floored "nightclub" is the essence of existence. Thus, this guide is aimed at those young people thinking of or already attending university. By following these instructions, a member of the younger generation can maintain his respect and be looked upon by the general public as an example of unbridled panache and *élan*, rather than a tax-dodging, bedizened loafer.

There is, of course, only one university in Britain, and that is Oxford. Many other cities and towns claim that they also have similar establishments, but a true Chap would blush from spending three of his formative years in some concrete monstrosity of the Midlands, or the dark satanic mills of the North. One is not to be fooled either by members of the royal family who opt to join the arts-and-craft communities of our Caledonian cousins. Intelligent homosexuals are permitted to attend the University of Cambridge, which offers a variety of courses on espionage leading to worthy careers working for the KGB in mysterious buildings south of the Thames.

Oxford, as you are doubtless aware (but those you wish to influence may not be), is made up of a number of colleges, and it is essential to choose appropriately. Otherwise one will be mired in some Stygian examination-factory full of northern scholars and other low personages, and one will but hear rumours of gentle sophistication, and occasionally catch a glimpse of fine fellows clad in finest tweed in retreat from lecture theatres in search of splendid beverages. Christ Church and Keble come highly recommended, Keble particularly, as it has high church connections, which always come in useful when explaining one's actions to the magistrate. Lincoln is also tolerable, and possibly Magdalen (although our old scout warns us that they admit what he calls "grungy sorts" as well these days). If these fail, then St John's, Trinity, University, Worcester and St Benet's Hall will suffice, although you will be in a minority, and must treat your time there much as a nineteenth century missionary would have in attempting to spread the Chappist credo. Sadly, even Oxford has its hotbeds of all-embracing radicalism and rent strikes

An undergraduate should ensure that his modest accomodation is furnished in a style that befits a gentleman.

of Symbolist poetry. If one's finances run to it, employ an amusing dwarf to pass round the cocktails; but if one is financially embarrassed, make do with a pet badger with a tray of canapés strapped to its back.

A minuscule proportion of your time at these temples of education could be spent desperately trying to complete assessments or cram for examinations, so it is essential to chose a course that will pose no intellectual challenge whatsoever (and where you may also meet like-minded gentlemen). Therefore, at all costs, one must choose an Arts subject that one is already vaguely knowledgeable about. No interesting books have been written since Mr Rider Haggard's splendid *King Solomon's Mines* in 1885, so English literature is unlikely to expand in the near future. Likewise History has remained fairly stagnant since the Relief of Mafeking. Foreign languages are also a gentle option, as it matters not if one graduates without being able to speak a word of a foreign lingo, *The Chap* having recently begun a policy of scattering copies of this august publication overseas. Therefore not only will Johnny Foreigner speak the Chap's English, he will also be able to advise on the nearest establishment where one's moustache can be appropriately waxed.

The sciences are to be avoided at all costs. Not only are they exceedingly difficult and require a gentleman to spend inordinate amounts of time in a laboratory staring blankly at the periodic table, but also one will be surrounded by the strangest sort of creature one would fear to meet. These fellows (there are no ladies in the world of the scientist) will have a complexion that appears never to have seen sunlight, hair that has never been in contact with a barber's implements, nor even a plunge of brilliantine, and their garb will consist of ill-fitting black "t-shirts" bearing extraordinary messages, such as "Napalm Death" or shiny acrylic garments bearing the legend "Sunderland FC". A true chap will never gain a degree in science, as the horror of these forced-upon companions will send him fleeing from the building to settle in a dingy cellar for three years' contemplation with the hookah.

which must be avoided at all costs: for example Pembroke, and to some extent Wadham, Somerville, Exeter, Hertford and Queen's. Balliol can have its over-enthusiastic students, but has enough of a tweed-clad contingent to make it bearable.

On arrival at one's college, one must immediately redecorate one's rooms with black leather wallpaper, peacock fathers, a sheaf of assegais over the chimneypiece, several daguerreotypes of oneself on safari, a collection of shrunken heads, a Nantucket harpoon ("went whaling in me gap year") and leather-bound, travel-bruised editions of 'Sapper', John Buchan, Biggles, "artistic" magazines, Thesiger (Ernest, not Wilfred) and volumes

The main dangers to which one's dignity will be exposed will come from other people. Sadly, as ever in this brave new world, not everyone lives on a diet of couth manners, esoteric literature and impressive liqueurs, and at university one will be exposed to these others, therefore one should choose one's friends with more care than normal. When joining societies, it is imperative that future implications are considered. What may at first seem like an elegant collection of young gentlemen of the Hellfire Society may soon become a pathetic collection of pock-marked specimens comparing episodes of American television programmes set in outer space and bemoaning the continuation of their virginity. However, when one inevitably becomes President of the Union, using nefarious methods made traditional by the least civilised members of the Empire, the opportunity to surround oneself with the most sparkling minds, and perhaps a dazzling lady to make the tea and begin your biography, will present itself. It is at this point that one will require the elimination of the dreadful fellows that were met during the early days of term, with their "I did rather well in my A-levels, two Cs and a D"; "after Coventry I went travelling to Leicester, but it's simply too commercial and popular these days, so we hitched to Derby and travelled there for a while" and "I do miss my mum, I want to go home, where's teddy?"

Should the Chap not wish to attend Oxford the only other establishments worth frequenting are the Universities of Heidelberg and Ruritania. At the former one can obtain duelling scars, blood-brotherhood, Palatinate beer and flaxen-haired maidens; at the latter one can wear funny hats, partake in comic-opera revolutions, and end up as Minister of Culture (where one can make statutory the Noonday Absinthe Power Nap). Do not make the mistake of going to the Sorbonne. Instead of sipping a Pastis and swapping *bons mots* with Henri de Montherlant, one will find oneself ripping up the agreeable cobblestones of the Boul' Mich' and lobbing them at blue-chinned riot police – scarcely the way a gentleman wishes to spend his education.

At the end of the academic year, one will spend a few hours in a fractious hall easing through the examinations, where, in three hours, one will produce more written work than has been done in the whole of the previous nine months. Contrary to advice, one should never read the exam questions too closely, but simply write all that one knows about a particular subject, and assume that, in the midst of it, a fusty academic will discover that you are far too clever for his silly questions and award you the highest mark imaginable.

The true *ur*-Chap will, however, never set foot in an examination hall, having contrived to be rusticated mid-way through his final year for stoning the college swan to death with empty gin bottles.

A YEAR IN CATFORD

Provençal vignerons DIDIER and
VERONIQUE CAUDILLON have
exchanged the rural idyll of their
farmhouse in Aix-en-Provence for
an authentic South London council
flat. This is the second instalment
of their diary for an unforgettable
year in Catford, London SE6

The Gault-Millau guide to Britain describes Fran's Kitchen on Catford High Street as "an authentic South London 'greasy spoon café', ideal for lingering Sunday breakfasts. If you can leave the establishment after Fran's Gutbuster Special Breakfast without medical assistance, you should ask for a refund." It sounded delightful. We entered Fran's kitchen unsteadily, still queasy from the previous night's *divertissements*. We were, however, conscious that our bodies were beginning to adapt to *Le Style Catfordois*. We could now drink six or seven pints of Fosters and share a pack of Benson & Hedges without vomiting.

The eponymous Fran greeted us with an endearing grimace when we asked to see the menu, waving a tattooed arm at a blackboard behind the counter. The charmingly illiterate scrawlings offered various combination breakfasts, conveniently numbered for ease of ordering. Number One, for example, contained *oeufs frites*, *porc saucisson*, *champignons frites* marinated in melted lard, *tranches* of *porc fumé* and *haricots blancs* in a thick *sauce tomate*. However, this was chicken feed when one glanced down the menu at the final *piece de resistance*, Madame Fran's 'Gutbuster Special', which we both felt duty bound, as fearless epicurean explorers, to order.

We had to move to a larger table to accommodate the plates when our meals arrived. The main dish was piled high with various fried viands, kidneys, liver and a curious black *saucisson* that seemed to contain whatever remained of the pig. Side orders included a *fricassée* of *pommes de terre*, *chou* and *autres legumes de la poubelle*, as well as the familiar *frites Anglaises* and thick slices of butter on a *pain blanc* base.

As we hacked our way through this smorgasbord of carbohydrates, we understood how this peasant fare was the perfect antidote for our bodies, which the previous evening's mammoth session in the pub had reduced to a quivering mass of toxins, clamouring for release through our pores.

Strangely bloated yet entirely malnourished, we exited Fran's Kitchen into the bleak winter smog of South London. With our minds so befuddled that we could barely manage to converse with each other in French, let alone practise our South London patois, we were clearly in the perfect frame of mind for a visit to a DIY centre. The Gault-Millau guide recommends two such outlets: the Catford branch of Homebase ("the discerning DIY enthusiast will find all their homemaking needs under one glorious quasi-Palladian glass roof") and the nearby Bromley branch of B&Q ("to borrow from their advertising jingle, *si vouz voulez-y faire, vouz le devrais B&Quaire*").

We had clearly picked up on a Catford tradition, for the car park of Homebase was positively heaving with four-wheel drives. Shaven-headed men, their flabby necks sagging with resignation, trailed into the building after their snarling, peroxided wives and their tattooed offspring, all clad in matching football shirts. This family expedition was evidently a form of worship; the Sunday service *de nos jours*.

Our research into current South London interior design modes had been bountiful, since doing up one's home appeared to be *en vogue* at the moment, with a variety of television programmes devoted to it. We saw that the key to *Le Style Anglais* lay in materials. So we purchased MDF by the truckload, slabs of Formica, some linoleum tiles, some cheap, synthetic carpet tiles, large tins of magnolia emulsion paint and a selection of charming garden gnomes. Our two-bedroom council flat on the Dregnor Estate was not in possession of a garden, nor even a balcony, but the television programmes had given us some bright ideas to overcome such a handicap.

First of all, the kitchenette. An all-over coat of beige emulsion paint soon obliterated the scorch marks and knife holes left by the previous tenants. We gave the room a gritty urban feel by painting the furniture beige as well, as well as all the cupboards and the kettle and toaster. Taking our cue from *"Changons Chambres!"*, we then stencilled some atmospheric words in large type around the walls: PIES, BEER, CHIPS, PICKLED ONIONS,

BANGERS, CHOCOLATE HOB NOBS. "Fran's Kitchen, eat your heart out!" we joked as we painted them on.

When it came to the living room, it was clear that a radical rethink was required. The previous tenants had not done much with it, apart from allowing their dog to chew up most of the carpet. The room was a bit of a nondescript box, so the solution clearly lay in partitioning. We set to work with MDF and a jigsaw to create an environment that would reflect our cultural surroundings.

Le Petit Pub, as we liked to call it, occupied a quarter of the room when it was completed. It had all the attributes of a real South London pub – a sticky bar, watered-down draught beer, horse brasses, thudding music, a bloodstained floor. We would take it in turns to serve each other drinks, performing amusing caricatures of our favourite publicans to practise our *Catfordois*. At the opposite end of the room we constructed a kebab stall. This had an ersatz meat spit as its central feature (built ingeniously from chicken wire and cardboard), a flickering neon sign saying 'Best Doner', and a salad bar, which we lent an air of authenticity by only cleaning very occasionally and leaving the salad to wither in Tupperware trays.

For the remainder of the flat we achieved a *Catfordois* feel by pebbledashing the walls and crazy-paving the hallway. Water features were '*dans*' apparently, so we bought a second-hand bidet and cemented it ironically outside the bathroom, placing a garden gnome with a fishing rod where the taps had been. Oh, how our Provençal neighbours would have seethed with envy! The centrepiece for a Catford living room, as we gathered from the profusion of satellite dishes covering our block, was the television set. Although we had already installed one in every other room in the flat, it was evident that to achieve the correct note of authenticity, the living room would have to possess *la mère de toutes les televisions*.

In Provence, when you need a new cow or a flock of sheep, the purchasing process takes an entire day – a very enjoyable day at the cattle market usually involving an enormous five-course meal with one of the livestock owners, with the documentation signed over a glass of fifteen-year-old Armagnac. We imagined that purchasing a television set in South London would be a similarly grand event.

The Catford branch of Currys electronic goods emporium is one of the largest in the country. Its very impressive array of merchandise includes a staggering fifteen different types of microwave, as one of the assistants informed us while leading us to the televisual department. Aniil, as the charming young man's nameplate described him, was extremely informative on the joys of cable television, if a little rusty on how to plug the set in. It was soon clear that we were going to learn much about the local culture once we had a satellite dish installed. Aniil flicked through some of the ninety or so channels that would be available to us, and we caught tantalizing glimpses of programmes devoted to shopping, quiz shows, darts, snooker, football and soap operas. The television set, for the typical *Catfordois*, is a veritable portal on to the rich tapestry of world culture. No wonder there are so few travel agents in the area: the locals have no need of international travel, for they can learn all they need to know of the world at the flick of a switch.

There was no offering of Armagnac while Aniil whirred our credit card through the processing machine, but he had made an effort to be sociable. We spontaneously invited him to the *crémaillère* that were planning for the following evening. This was to combine showing off our new décor and TV set with meeting some of the neighbours again.

With Christmas just around the corner, we decided to provide some yuletide fare for our party. We anticipated

around thirty guests, so a trip to Lidl was in order to stock up on the necessary victuals. Since most people would have lots of parties to go to around Christmas, we thought we should also make some invitations. "Didier and Veronique Caudillon request the pleasure of your company at 7 pm on Thursday 22nd December for a Noël repast. We shall also be glad to share the delights of our brand-new 96-inch Panasonic widescreen colour television set with Plasma screen and Dolby surround sound. Dress code: elegant, festive. RSVP by 8th December." We had thirty invitations printed on violet vellum with a gold edge, decorated with some embossed images of Christmas trees and television sets. Having distributed most of them among the residents of Dregnor Estate, we sat back and waited for the RSVPs to return.

By Wednesday 21st we had not had a single response, so we assumed that perhaps RSVP was not as typical a custom as we thought. However, a few discreet knocks on doors soon revealed how shy some of our neighbours were! "Are you coming to the party tomorrow night?" we asked, wearing coloured paper hats and waving Christmas crackers as a temptation. One of the neighbours, a youthful Jamaican fellow, got into the spirit of things by pointing a toy gun at us through the bars that covered his front door. We took his muttered reply to be a 'perhaps'. But other neighbours expressed enthusiasm, especially when we mentioned the new television. The words 'Plasma Screen' appeared to be some sort of Shibboleth.

The designated hour finally came, and suddenly the doorbell began ringing. It didn't stop until well past nine, and soon the flat was packed with more people than we thought we had invited. The dress code, in quaint South London fashion, had been interpreted quite imaginatively – most of the guests were wearing tracksuits, except for one old fellow who came in his pyjamas.

Having closely observed the other shoppers in Lidl, we had created what we took to be the typical *Catfordois* Christmas meal. The hors d'oeuvres consisted of *roulade de saucisson* with *frites a la fromage et ognion* and *brochettes de fromage et ananas* on cocktail sticks. The main course was deep-fried *nuggets de dinde* with *Frites McCain au four* smothered in

aioli and *sauce tomate.* Dessert was *petites tartes aux fruits dégueulasses* and *chocolats de la Rue de Qualité.*

We had planned some Christmas party games, but most of the guests were keen to watch the new television, so we tried to find a channel that suited everyone. This was difficult, and several fracas broke out over whether to watch the Discovery Channel documentary about sharks or some repeats of *EastEnders* on UK Gold. We secretly wanted to watch *Jean de Florette* on Film Four, hoping to share some of our own culture with the neighbours, but this was soon outvoted by a show of fists, and even something we took to be a death threat from one rather over-refreshed fellow.

Unfortunately, agreement could not be reached, and at one o'clock in the morning arguments were still raging over which of the soap operas was superior. Fairly tired by now after an day of cooking and putting up Christmas decorations, we suggested a Christmas toast with Southern Comfort as a subtle way of wishing our guests good night.

By five o'clock, there were still around forty people in the flat. Perhaps offering to continually replenish the supply of lager from the all-night Turkish supermarket had been a mistake, particularly in the case of the unfortunate lady who had been unable to contain herself on the kitchen floor, but we felt at least that we had got to know our neighbours more intimately.

After finally closing the door on the last of the guests at five-thirty in the morning, we sat on our enormous leatherette sofa to reflect on our first Christmas in Catford. The first thing we noticed was that where the television set had been, there was now an empty space on the carpet. Oh well, we surmised, one of the neighbours must have mistaken it for their own. How silly of them, but then all these flats must look more or less identical. It was a testament to what an authentically *Catfordois* feel we had achieved with our interior decoration.

CATFORDOIS – A BLUFFER'S GUIDE

FANCY A PINT?	UNE PETIT PASTIS?
LOOK AT THE TITS ON THAT!	AH, QUELLE JEUNE FILLE SI BELLE!
HE'S ON THE ROCK 'N' ROLL	IL A BESOIN D'ASSISTANCE ECONOMIQUE DE LA GOUVERNEMENT
OUT OF THE WAY, ARSEHOLE!	CHANGEZ VOTRE POSITION, S'IL VOUS PLAIT!
WOTCHEW LUKINAT MATE?	EST—CE QUE VOUS AVEZ VU QUELQUE CHOSE INTERESSANT, MON AMI?
TEN QUID? YER 'AVIN A LARF, INNIT?	VOTRE PRIX EST TRES AMUSANT POUR VOUZ, MAIS PAS POUR MOI!
FARKIN' WANKER!	VOUS ETES UN VERITABLE ONANISTE, MONSIEUR!

FITNESS ELAN. We consulted that dissolute PE instructor and disgraced headmaster Marmaduke Dedalus on the correct levels of physical fitness for a gentleman to attain. "Fiddlesticks!" he bellowed from his home-made wigwam on the periphery of Eton's playing fields. Here are Mr Dedalus's Dos and Don'ts of keeping fit.

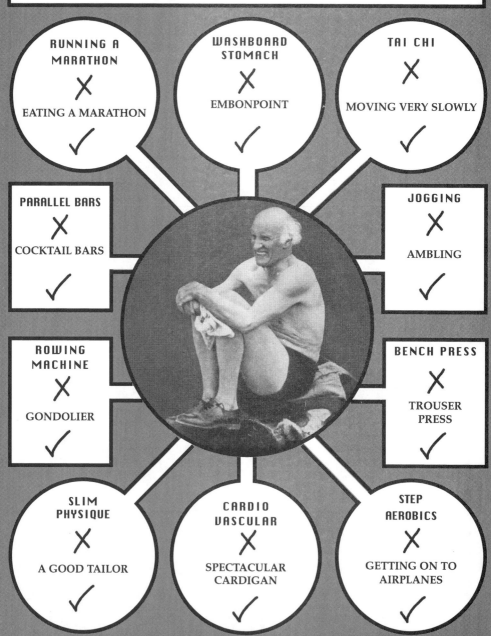

RUNNING A MARATHON
✗
EATING A MARATHON
✓

WASHBOARD STOMACH
✗
EMBONPOINT
✓

TAI CHI
✗
MOVING VERY SLOWLY
✓

PARALLEL BARS
✗
COCKTAIL BARS
✓

JOGGING
✗
AMBLING
✓

ROWING MACHINE
✗
GONDOLIER
✓

BENCH PRESS
✗
TROUSER PRESS
✓

SLIM PHYSIQUE
✗
A GOOD TAILOR
✓

CARDIO VASCULAR
✗
SPECTACULAR CARDIGAN
✓

STEP AEROBICS
✗
GETTING ON TO AIRPLANES
✓

LETTERS

SIR,

Following a freak windmill accident on the Suffolk Borders, I have recently had cause to be amputated from the eyebrows down. Naturally I am fitted with the very latest design in torso-prosthetics. However, I find myself somewhat limited with regards to my choice of gentlemen's frippery and attire. Walter suggests various ideas involving velour flannels and 'velcro' or some such fad. But we all know what an overblown oaf he is. As befits my situation, I do find myself focusing upon the 'Decorative Arts of the Eyebrow', and I was curious as to whether I might rely on you fellows of fine taste to recommend a reputable Eyebrow Powderer in the South London area?

Yours in brow-furrowing anticipation,
ETHELRED HEDGEROW-HEDGEROW

DEER SJRS,

I am Norwegian living in Engerland and are cross about David Saxby's jeering at us in your Issue 14. He makes unkind remarks about 'lego reindeer', but you ask me; where would your English Christmas be without our reindeer? And where would English children be without Norwegian Lego? Ha! I break my fingers at you. Also at our national dress he cast asparagus. I, for one, do not have reindeer on my jumper. We come from fishing folk and my Greta she put cod pieces all over. David Saxby would cry to see it.

So, Saxby think foreigners amusing. I bet he don't find this amusing.

BJORN UPYRBUUM.

SIR,

I fully empathise with Major Bulmer Bag-Puisse (issue 15) and the vexing badger question. My friends and I recently gathered for one of our Bacchanalian rites within my woodlands. At the point of ritual consummation with a brace of Dorset Naiads, in an ecstasy of squealing, I was surrounded by an incandescent, unearthly light shed from some hovering aerial eye – a machine I later discovered to be called a helicopter. Within minutes our merry band was corralled by burly men of a humourless countenance, clad in what I believe is known as 'body armour'. "Are you badger baiting, sir?" I was asked.

In reply, I snorted "I object strongly to your reference to my gals as members of the mustelidae family and may the curse of Actaeon be upon you for spying on us." They pressed a very unwelcome invitation on us to make the acquaintance of some body known as the Weymouth Magistrates Court. I may decline the invitation as we are engaged that week in the removal of thistles at groin height from the downland where we hold our ritual bull sacrifice every Autumnal equinox.

CLAUDIUS BEAUCHAMP,
BUCKLAND RIPERS, DORSET

SIR,

Cephalogically speaking, Mr Hussein's approach to world domination may be flawed. No dictator worth his salt would wear a Homburg, surely?

JOHN MORRIS,
OFFICIAL MONSTER RAVING LOONY PARTY

SIR,
While lunching at the Savoy last Wednesday, I overheard a bunch of finely dressed young coves engaged in talk best left for the robe room of a gymnastic establishment or some such place, for they were discussing the whys, the wherefores and the whatsitsnames of Greco-Roman wrestling. At the Savoy! At luncheon! Well, I'm afraid I simply could not bring myself to remain there for my Citrus Tart with Fruity Sauce. I donned my hat and left the damned place forthwith, nose erect. My question to you is this: from whence do today's rum bucks learn such Communist behaviour?

SIR RATHBONE SMYTHE SMYTHE-SMYTHE

SIR,
I would just like to show support as a lady reader, and let all you chaps know that us women too indulge in your magazine, or how else could we turn you into such fine gentlemen? On my travels, I decided to take my Chap for a walk along the Great Wall of China, since a lady should really be accompanied along the way.

LADY PENELOPE PEMBERTON, SURREY

SIR,
Some months ago I noted that we were to be treated to a series of televisual vignettes entitled 'Pop Idle'. Imagine my disappointment when, instead of enjoying insights into the lives of dandily-attired young blades at their leisure and ageing roués draped in petticoated young ladies, we were insulted by scenes of spike-haired castrati and loud mouthed, large breasted northern girls auditioning for the end of the pier show. I strongly suspect that somebody had been tampering with the producer's laudanum and hope that he fulfils his remit for a new concatenation of tableaux entitled 'Pop Idle – the Revels' with more responsibility to his viewers.

Yours wounded by calumny,
JM SOUTHCOTT

SIRS,
I spent several days in the British Museum Reading Room toiling with matters of Byzantine merkinry. It appears an irregularity known to the modern merkinoisie as 'Bishop's Perambulatory Scratch' was virtually eradicated by the ancient scholars of sartoria-genitum. Such an 'irritation' to the day-to-day 'going about' of the Gentleman would never, it seems, have been allowed to persist even amongst the lower orders of Byzantine society. It occurs to me that various behavioural irregularities and social faux pas might very well be explained away by a Gentleman's suddenly becoming gripped about his 'person' by 'The Scratch'. It is surely beyond the wit of any man to remain upstanding in his elegance whilst overcome with a feeling of 'bareback thornbush equestrianism'.

The next time one encounters an episode of questionable behaviour, perhaps it might be of humanitarian duty to remove 'the offender' to one side and gently massage the 'vicinité merkinoise' until a degree of order is restored. If such treatment fails, the man can be unashamedly lampooned and bombasted in front of all and sundry whilst one takes the credit for having singled out the unabashed buffoon.

With warm regards,
SIR BEATRICE WARDROBE-WARDROBESHIRE

THE CHAP QUESTIONNAIRE

Earl Okin

Poet, singer, guitarist, pianist and comedian Earl Okin has been playing his intensely personal form of the bossa nova since the 1960s, including a sensational 18-year run at the Edinbrugh Festival. The Earl is also something of a hit with the ladies, who are often surprised to hear such a Nat King Cole-like voice from a man who wears spats and drives a Rover 95. His debut gramophone recording, Musical Genius & Sex Symbol, is out now on Sony Jazz.

What is your idea of complete sophistication?
I like my man to serve tiffin in the back seat of my Rover 95, two satin-clad beauties sitting either side of me, tempting me with petits-fours. The chauffeur has been trained to drive slowly at this time, lest the cream curdles.

Who, in your opinion, is or was the quintessential English gentleman?
It's really a toss up between David Niven and myself, I suppose.

And the quintessential lady?
Dame Clara Butt. Over six-foot tall and when she sang 'Land Of Hope & Glory', the Royal Albert Hall shuddered! What a fine nanny she would have made...

Where do you think the best-dressed people are?
Well, you know. I have this little club I go to. Nothing overdone, you understand, but everything is done in the greatest taste and the people who go along are, well, the right sort and know just what to wear for all occasions.

Name three favourite items in your wardrobe.
My grey bowler hat; my silver-topped cane and my silver half-hunter and fob. Silver is far less garish than gold, don't you think? Gold makes a chap look foreign!

What items of clothing do you consider to be the height of vulgarity?
T-shirts and jeans. I won't have either item in my wardrobe.

What single situation has been the greatest challenge to your wardrobe and your grooming skills?
Changing the tyre on my Rover in a force 9 gale, the very night when Sevenoaks became ThreeTwigs. Unfortunately, my man had the night off.

Which accessories would you never venture into polite society without?
One should never EVER venture forth without one's spats.

Which aspects of contemporary life do you think are most prohibitive of a gentlemanly lifestyle?
Any motor car without a starting handle and walnut interior.

How do you think young people can be prevented from becoming sportswear-clad ruffians?
A three-year apprenticeship in Savile Row. Any establishment there ought to do.

What vices, if any, do you believe are conducive to beauty of mind and independence of spirit?
The playing of pre-war gramophone records on a well preserved Columbia 1928 Grafonola...using LOUD needles...at any time of day or night.

Which view from which window would you describe as "a portal to the sublime"?
The window of my Rover 95. Who cares where I am driving...it's that window that counts! Ah, they really used to know how to make a motor-car window!

2004

5

CHAPTER

LETTERS

SIR,

Upon reading in your article 'Alumnus Elegantis' (issue 16) that Cambridge offers courses in espionage for homosexuals, I am immediately applying for a place. I am slightly concerned about the espionage, however. Is it very onerous? Would one be required to go to Russia, and if so where is it? Would you know whether any of the colleges offer homosexuality and Leisure Studies, which might be more suited to my abilities?

Your most obedient servant,
ALGERNON 'KIM' PHILPOTTS.

SIR,

I must protest in the strongest possible terms at the letter from Lady Penelope Pemberton. As a 'modern man' I encourage the ladies to read *The Chap* and welcome their comments – but dash it all, how can a lady travel the Far East in garb that is calculated to confuse natives who expect the highest decorum from the English. What are the coolies to make of a white woman wearing someone's trousers, and carrying a satchel. And the woman is not wearing a hat!!! It would not surprise me to learn that she was something to do with the bus conductors' outing shown in the background of her picture.

MAJOR BULMER BAG-PUISSE
BAG PUISSE NORTON, WILTSHIRE.

P.S. I wonder if her mother was Lady "Raleigh" Pemberton, so-called for reasons best not mentioned.

SIRS,

On a recent restorative jaunt eastward, to enjoy the usual hedonistic and peculiarly greasy-haired delights of the Communist mainland of Europe, I encountered a rather strange bedfellow.

I packed up the motor vehicle with the requisite sundry items a gentleman might call upon, such as whalebone nasal spatulas, Laminated Whores and the like, and took flight to Dover. On arrival en grenouille, I drove masterfully with side-mouthed snarl and scant regard for local regulatory bothers, to my favourite resting place. Ah, the mythic joy of Le Blaireau Monoclé! But, to my horror, upon surrendering my drained grande-touriste self to the perfumed ivoire sheets of Le Blaireau's queen-sized, I became the latest victim of Communist tittle-tattle. Not wishing to remain a statistic without a cause, I decided upon voicing my outrage to you good fellows.

As a result of the latest plot of Euro World Domination, I experienced the abject terror of the collapsible pillow. No sooner did my vexed cranium hit the damned thing, than I found myself replete with two scantily eiderdowned jowls. Upon attempting to struggle free I merely became further entrenched, and began witnessing snippets of past escapades, which whilst thoroughly enjoyable, and only serving to remind me of what a damn fine egg I always have been, indicated to me that I was fast approaching death. I employed my robust nature and leapt free in a maniacal fit of fortitude. Wheezing, and sporting a side-parting not fit for a Belgian shower curtain salesman,

I stormed down to reception in disgust. Whyfore do the local peasantry suffer such crippling taxation, if we dandy types are not to benefit from the public services they yield? The whole heretical 'Euro project' is surely doomed to failure. I have recently joined my local town-twinning association, where I have uncovered a delicious plot of covert colonisation, not to mention a furtive interest in Miss Hearthwarming. A photographic plate is enclosed for your perusal.

ERNEST FERRETTER

SIR,
I thought it would interest your readers to hear of my recent travels in the barren expanses of Tibet. Having decided to reach the forbidden city of Lhasa by yak, dressed up as a man – this to avoid undue attention from the most uncouth of the region's inhabitants – I set off from the exotic incense-swathed streets of Kathmandu, setting my course to the north. I had attached to my service a young and able-bodied sherpa servant boy, who soon took a keen interest in the few copies of *The Chap* I had taken care of packing in my light travelling bag. Soon he was proficient in the art of waxing my moustache and helping me dress in a proper gentlemanly fashion, which ensured I was not discovered as we crossed deserted plains and encountered gruff but gentle nomads herding their cattle below frozen glaciers. My young friend was especially helpful in the bandaging of my supple, firm breasts, which would have given my gender away without proper compression.

I am attaching to this letter a picture of my excellent manservant holding a copy of your magazine atop a most treacherous Tibetan pass, from which most of the Himalayas can be beheld, stretching as far as the eye can see, looming in the unforgiving horizon.

I trust you will be happy to know that I have taken this quite astounding pupil back to England, where I have ensured he is clothed in the latest Savile Row fashion, and where I keep on teaching him the manners befitting a British gentleman, as well as how to attend to me thoroughly during my hot scented baths.

JUSTINE "BILL" FARNSWORTH
LAMBETH, LONDON

Howard Spent investigates

THE PHYSIOGNOMY OF
THE KNAVE

I n this issue it is my unpleasant task to turn away from the usual varied diet provided by these pages of insight, and instead invite you to dine upon a restricted and rather unpalatable menu. My semiotic investigations naturally lead me into contact with many manner of man both decent fellow and irretrievable bounder, but this quarter, Dear Reader, I intend to take a walk on the dark side and concentrate solely on those cads, rotters, and criminal types that are unfortunately encountered in all walks of life.

"How", I hear you ask, "are we to identify these miscreants so that we can be pre-warned of their skulduggery?" Contrary to popular belief they do not all wear striped T-shirts, face masks and carry hessian sacks with the word 'swag' written upon them. Believe it or not, some of these ne'er-do-wells look very much like you or me. In fact some do their best to merge with the crowd in order to facilitate their wrong-doings. Luckily, the trained eye of the semiotician can prove sturdy weapon against this decidedly motley shower.

It is impossible to be a scoundrel or a knave without the facial features giving the fact away. Felonious intent will be written, albeit with great subtlety, into every crevice, every movement and every pore of a criminal's visage. This will either occur through the ravages of a criminal's lifetime (wasn't it George Orwell who once wrote: 'A man at 50 has the face he deserves'?) or, alternatively, by

the action of genetic mutation over many generations. A man who has spent countless years relieving little old ladies of their life's savings, for example, will ultimately experience hardening of the corners of the mouth and the development of hooded, cold eyes akin to those of a bird of prey. On the other hand, those with a congenital predisposition for street crime such as a muggers, pick pockets or traffic wardens, will have been born possessing the protuberant brow and lolloping gait of the Neanderthal.

It should be be noted at this point, by contrast, acts of kindness such as missionary work introducing school children to the benefits of tobacco products can lead to nothing other than an untroubled countenance of saintly beauty. In the final analysis, no matter whether a fellow is born with the telltale signs of knavery or acquires them over the course of time, to the observant eye, a villain's countenance is as incriminating as a signed affidavit.

Over the next few pages there follows a rogues gallery of personages one would rather not meet down a darkened alley in the early hours of the morning and whom one would rather walk to the opposite side of the public thoroughfare than to pass in close proximity. I humbly submit a summary of my findings to you, in the hope they will keep you safe and sound on your law-abiding way. I am sure you will find that they will prove an invaluable guide for use socially, in business, and for pleasure.

The Card Sharp

Neurosis about his unattractive chin and sunken eyes has caused this fellow to spend hours alone in his bedroom learning the techniques of prestidigitation. He should face the facts, card tricks are the closest he is ever likely to get to actually 'finding the lady'.

The Mule

Identifiable by a long face and big trusting eyes, this fellow is the work horse of the world of crime. He is willing to smuggle contraband such as soap to France or MacDonald's burgers to Colombia to finance his addiction to the granular white stuff.

The Street Ruffian

With a brow reminiscent of the Continental Shelf and a countenance indicative of base thuggery, this specimen may still sidestep a life of penal servitude by changing his name and attempting to convince the world that he is a passable actor.

The Nark

This police informer is in a quandary as to where his loyalties lie. Even a criminal should remain true to his friends. Untrustworthiness coupled with indecision can lead to excessive hair growth between the eyebrows and unattractive flaring in the nostril region.

The Lady of Ill Repute

The 15th Earl of Camardenshire might believe that he is fulfilling his 'artistic' destiny by employing collagen and silicon to mimic the charms of Miss Marilyn Monroe, but, in actual fact, he is guilty of the most heinous felonies against the laws of Madam Nature.

The Errand Boy

This angelic-looking cove's winning smile and tousled locks indicate a willingness to be led by others. He has consequently fallen in with a bad crowd and now finds his foot firmly set on the first rung of the ladder of infamy – running errands for Mr Big.

The Flasher

Sex perverts and other trouser-related offenders are renowned for possessing oddly striated facial features. Shown on numerous television crime programmes, one would think that this singular-looking blackguard would have been apprehended long ago.

The Extortionist

With an upper lip stretched tightly over an unctuous grin and a livid scar upon his cheek, this blighter is obviously a cold-hearted hoodlum well-versed in trickery and deceit. Many years with the mob have prepared him well for his new career in estate agency.

The Brigand

Although his salty dog's weathered face and shifty eyes speak of plunder and pillage, he might still avoid the attentions of the constabulary if it were not for his insistence on wearing a distinctive hat whilst on shoplifting expeditions to his local supermarket.

The Bully Boy

Insecurity about one's facial hair statement can lead to gross distortions of a man's character. This swarthy miscreant's unstylish tash has caused him to be utterly beastly to his work colleagues and neighbours. He is richly deserving of an immense thrashing.

The Mastermind

His determined mouth could mark this man out as a global operator of immense intellect, but the mutual proximity of his eyes tells an entirely different tale. It should be remembered that idiocy is not regarded as a legitimate defence in an international court of law.

The Hooligan

A visage grotesquely twisted into the mask of a clown demonstrates to all and sundry that this buffoon is an avid follower of the game of 'football'; but beware, eight pints of lager could turn this harmless imbecile into a weapon of mass destruction.

A YEAR IN CATFORD

Provençal vignerons DIDIER and
VERONIQUE CAUDILLON have
exchanged the rural idyll of their
farmhouse in Aix-en-Provence for
an authentic South London council
flat. This is the third instalment of
their diary for an unforgettable
year in Catford, London SE6

T
he Gault-Millau Guide du
Bretagne describes the menu
of the Catford Greyhound
Stadium snack bar as "the
very heart and soul of
Catfordois peasant fare. The visiting gour-
mand will find it difficult to choose from
Hot Dogs (par-boiled *saucisson du gras*
with pork traces, drizzled with *sauce
tomate* and *moutarde Anglaise*, served in a
brioche ancienne), Scampi and Chips
(breaded goujons of *poisson pour le chat*
with a *garni* of *salade tiede d'hier*) or
Hamburger and Chips (*faux filet haché
dans une bap grillée avec frites Anglaises*)
and he will have to return to the Dog stadium on several consecutive evenings simply in order to sample
the delicious menu in its entirety."

It was not only the culinary delights of the Catford Dogs that tempted us towards the stadium, but also
the sport of it. In Provence, the only sport which had figured in our lives was the annual goat race at
Bonnieux – and the real reason for attending that was the excellent Restaurant de la Gare in the village.
Here in south London, dog racing seemed to embody the very essence of *la vie Catfordois*: an exciting
communal experience pitting one man's mathematical predictions against another man's highly trained
four-legged beast. The day we chose to attend the races it was raining, in the persistent, unrelenting way
it only ever rains in south London. By the time we set out from Dregnor House at 6.30, the roadworks lining Catford Broadway had reduced the pavements to billowing rivulets of mud. This didn't do much for
our outfits, which we had chosen specifically to enter into the spirit of the racetrack, and consisted of hefty

tweeds, woollen overcoats and jaunty eight-section tweed caps. It wasn't until we arrived at the stadium and mingled with the other punters that we understood the difference between dog racing and horse racing.

The approach to Catford Greyhound Stadium has something of the ancient and mythical about it. As one mounts the steps of the railway bridge from Doggett Road, the stadium gradually spreads out before one's eyes. One is immediately reminded of the splendour of the Coliseum at Rome. Even the tower of neon over the entrance gates reading CATFOR TADIUM (some of the letters had short-circuited in the rain) read like a portentous Latin proclamation heralding some splendid and bloody tournament. Over the graffiti-covered metal walls of the bridge we could see the track itself, a dun-coloured loop of sand around the terraces. The hopes, dreams and *grandes illusions* of *Les Catfordois Sportifs* could be imagined blowing across that track like so many grains of sand, illuminated by the glare of the floodlights for a few brief hours, yet so soon to fade into the rain-lashed gloom of darkness.

Having absolutely no idea of the correct etiquette of the greyhound stadium, we took a few moments to observe the other punters in action. The stadium's various terraces all led up to a series of queues: one for the bar, one for the betting booth and one for the snack bar. The first port of call was, naturally, the bar; we observed that once each punter was furnished with a foaming pint of ale, he would proceed to the betting booth grasping his racecard and a pen. Having placed his bet, he would then join the food queue, and somehow manage to negotiate his way back to the terraces clutching a beer, a betting slip, a polystyrene tray of food and a mobile telephone, with only two arms and no tables to put anything on.

We followed suit and took our seats in the grandstand. The seats constituted the only wooden items in an edifice entirely composed of steel girders and concrete. This is what we love about British urban architecture – its stubborn functionality. Whereas in Provence a sporting venue would be full of aesthetic frills: wooden trellises with flowers, terracotta tiles on the floor, balconies with potted plants, wooden tables with checked tablecloths and candlesticks, here in Catford we sat huddled over a plastic tray of scampi in our laps and a pint of lager in our gloved hands.

But the races themselves were far too exciting for us to be distracted by our surroundings. As soon

as the six hounds had been released from their traps, the terraces erupted into a cacophony of thrilled exclamations from the punters. "Come on, the one/two/three/four/five/six dog!" was the principal exhortation being uttered towards the sinewy canines pounding after an ersatz hare, clearly enjoying the exercise after being cooped up in the back of a 4x4 all afternoon. The atmosphere was electric and overwhelming. Some of the men even stood up from their seats as the dogs approached the finishing line, some thirty seconds after beginning the race.

"Hard cheese, old mate!" I said to one disappointed-looking fellow as he tore up his betting slip. He gave me a brief reply that could have been "Thank you" and dived into the queue for the bar. Still unsure about the betting system – the race card seemed to contain nothing but a series of complicated numbers and fractions in very small type and some strange foreign-sounding names – we asked a jovial old fellow seated next to us for advice.

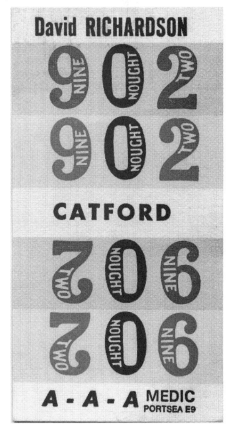

David RICHARDSON

902

902

CATFORD

206

206

A - A - A MEDIC
PORTSEA E9

"Could you explain the betting system to us, my old man?" I asked him.

"Let's get one thing straight, mate – I don't give tips, alright?" Evidently an old hand at these races, he explained that so many people had requested tips over the years that he had long ceased giving them, to avoid getting the flak for disappointing results.

"Yes, yes, yes, I quite understand," I said. "So which dog will win the next race?"

The man patiently explained the various qualities to look for in a dog to assess its winning potential, such as observing the position of its tail and keeping an eye on its bowel movements.

"So which dog will win the next race?" I asked. In my experience of British evasiveness, if one persists in asking them a direct question, they will eventually answer it.

"Limehouse Lad," said the old man under his breath, glancing about nervously. I descended the terrace and accosted a charming fellow under an umbrella next to the track, with a little blackboard behind him. "I believe that Limehouse Lad will be the winner," I said, proffering him a one-pound coin. The man quickly looked me up and down, then pointed to his blackboard which,

empty a moment ago, now read: 'Minimum bet £50'. "Oh well," I said, remembering a useful idiomatic expression for this situation, "in for a penny, in for fifty pounds." He smiled in what I thought was rather an insolent fashion and handed me a ticket.

When I went to rejoin Veronique she was no longer at our seats. The old man said she had been invited to join some local ladies for a drink. *C'est vraiment jolie*, I thought. It was high time Veronique made some friends in the area. For my part, I could already number a few of the local builders among my new acquaintances, but when I met them for a Saturday drink at the Green Man, it was made clear that the womenfolk were not invited. When the pub entertainment began, I could see why. Like all French ladies, Veronique has a fairly open mind about sexual matters, but even she would balk at the sight of two naked ladies smothered in baby oil, performing acts of lewdness upon each other in what is normally the Sunday carvery area of the Green Man.

I found Veronique at the bar, surrounded by a group of local ladies. Their unattractively rotund figures looked at odds with their faces, which displayed the poorly applied make-up and skin afflic-

tions of girls in their late teens. They wore many golden jewels upon their ears, wrists and fingers, and boasted such an assortment of dyed hairstyles that their heads collectively resembled an autumnal forest scene. Veronique introduced me to Shirley, Trixie, Kylie, Shazza, Trudi and Debs, all of whom were sporting similar tracksuits of a stretchy grey fabric. I couldn't help thinking how surprising it was that sportswear was manufactured in sizes so unsuited to physical exercise – unless these charming ladies had all purchased their tracksuits from the shot-putting range.

The conversation I had stepped into was on the theme of child rearing. It seemed that all of these women, in spite of their tender ages, had given birth to several offspring – indeed, some sported an identically grey-tracksuited infant at their sides, busily converting a polystyrene tray of chips into an ample midriff. Veronique and I are not altogether comfortable around children, seeing them mainly as hazards to our gourmandising and our interior design schemes. Even in France, where children are welcomed with open high chairs by most restaurants, we have observed with pity a small tyrant demolish its parents' luncheon by howling through the hors d'oeuvre and vomiting during the *trou Normand*. So when Veronique casually made reference to having volunteered our babysitting services to these ladies, I must have visibly blanched. But a wink from her told me what she was up to. Of course, I realised, having access to the homes of these local residents for entire evenings would give us thousands of new ideas for creating an authentic *Catfordois* interior to our own apartment.

Having exchanged telephone numbers, we took our leave from the ladies in time to observe the next race. Limehouse Lad came in 6th (out of six), having tripped over in the first lap. I asked the so-called expert what had gone wrong with his 'dead cert', and he explained that greyhounds often get what is known as 'track leg', making it difficult for them to take the corners of the track speedily. I thanked him for his helpful advice and explained that I was now experiencing 'track wallet', making it almost impossible for me to bet on any subsequent races.

We had a final pint of lager, standing on a carpet of muddy discarded betting slips, watching the steady February drizzle sluicing Catford's shattered dreams into the gutter. But the experience had been a valuable one.

PIPE SMOKER
OF THE
YEAR

T his year Stephen Fry won the
coveted title of Pipe Smoker
of the Year, an award created in 1964 by the The
Pipesmokers' Council to
honour a distinguished pipesmoker and
to raise money for charity. Mr Fry's
name now stands alongside such lumi-
naries as Sir Harold Wilson, Peter
Cushing, Sir Patrick Moore, Tony
Benn and Dave Lee Travis. *The Chap*
had the pleasure of meeting Mr Fry at
the lavish award ceremony at the
Savoy Hotel in London, where Gustav
Temple put some pertinent questions to him on the position, both
moral and political, of the pipe
smoker in modern society.

Mr Temple: What signals would you say are given out by smoking a pipe as opposed to smoking a cigarette?

Mr Fry: A pipe gives a man an air of authority and purpose. Unlike, say, the French, we British are ashamed to show any signs of individuality. Smoking a pipe marks one down as a dangerous eccentric, an image which most British people are not comfortable with. The French are unafraid of being perceived as bourgeois, so they will adopt external symbols of it such as pipes and hats quite readily.

Mr Temple: Can smoking a pipe be used as a seduction tool?

Mr Fry: Indeed. Many ladies are drawn to the image of a pipe smoker as a trustworthy, dependable individual. The patron saint of pipe smokers, Sherlock Holmes, has created an association between smoking a pipe and possessing mental acuity. Not only that, but the pipe also has pacific connotations, which the ladies find reassuring. There is nothing aggressive about a pipe.

Mr Temple: Is the use of a pipe clenched between one's teeth, as featured in many 1950s DIY manuals, conducive to manual labour?

Mr Fry: The pipe clenched between the teeth of the DIY enthusiast signals that he has put his boy racer days behind him and is ready to settle down. I personally would be inspired with far more confidence in a builder if he smoked a pipe. Then perhaps one wouldn't find so many roll-up butts scattered all over the floor when he has finished.

Mr Temple: Would you ever consider laying floorboards while smoking a pipe?

Mr Fry: I would rather smoke a pipe while watching someone else lay them.

Mr Temple: Would it make any sense to allow pipe smoking in zones where cigarettes are banned?

Mr Fry: There are certainly many restaurants which do not allow the smoking of a pipe, whereas they quite happily permit their customers to smoke cigarettes. Interestingly, it is more the *idea* of the pipe that such establishments fear. Once presented with the beautiful aroma of some choice tobacco, such restaurateurs soon lower their objections.

Mr Temple: What single situation in your life would have been far more pleasant if you had been in possession of your favourite pipe?

Mr Fry: Recently I have been directing a film, a very stressful process in itself, especially in pre-production. Everyone seems to be firing all manner of questions at me the whole time, expecting immediate answers – what colour tie, where should this go, and so forth. As was Harold Wilson's habit, I find the deployment of the pipe very useful as a way of gaining a few extra moments to consider my answer. If I begin the process of filling the bowl and lighting the pipe, I am not perceived as evading the question, and I am then able to give a satisfactory answer.

A YEAR IN CATFORD

Provençal vignerons DIDIER and VERONIQUE CAUDILLON have exchanged the rural idyll of their farmhouse in Aix-en-Provence for an authentic South London council flat. This is the fourth and final instalment of their diary of an unforgettable year in Catford, London SE6

The Gault-Millau Guide de Bretagne describes the Catford Ram as: "discreetly tucked away inside the Catford Centre, this charming little hostelry is a firm favourite with the *Catfordois* for a few hearty lunchtime pints and some gay banter. Darts are also played here. The pub sits on the fringes of the eloquent concrete bunker that is the Catford Centre. When viewed from Catford High Street, the stark lines of Arthur Headcorn's proto-Brutalist structure take the eye on a sweeping, unequivocal journey from the gargantuan feline gargoyle over the entrance to the centre's epicentre; its nucleus; its throbbing heart – Tesco Supermarket."

The Gault-Millau was spot on with its description: "As you take the 200-metre pilgrimage to this cut-price Mecca, you will find yourself waylaid by the temptations spilling out of the little stores that line your path: Poundstretcher, Bargains Galore, The Salvation Army Shop, Poundshack and Aladdins Cave. Long before you have reached Tesco, you will have filled your shopping basket with plastic buckets, novelty lighters, porcelain Navajo Indians, joss sticks, multi-packs of underpants, unusual storage solutions and dancing Santa Clauses."

Just when we thought we had finally made it to the shores of our oasis, and were about to waft through the splendid automatic doors of Tesco, we espied the last and most irresistible temptation on our journey. The Catford Ram abuts a branch of Iceland (a shop we have never fully understood), and is an ideal spot for the squires of Catford to take an ale or two and discuss the matters of the day, while the womenfolk fill their shopping carts with the victuals purveyed by the jolly tradesmen of Tesco.

Since we enjoy a more enlightened *marriage moderne*, the two of us share the shopping duties as well as the pleasures of gourmandising and ale supping. We passed through the swing doors of the Catford Ram, weighed down with our plastic purchases and eager for a tasty British pint. It took a few minutes to orientate ourselves, for the Ram, being windowless, is graced with an almost Hugoesque gloom. Typical for this corner of southeast London, the pub is disproportionately vast for its location, and therefore has the feeling of being almost empty. Apart from Veronique and the amply bosomed lady behind the bar, there was not a single female to be seen upon the premises.

"Good day to you, my dear," I said, quoting directly from the Gault-Millau glossary of colloquial English, "two flagons of your finest foaming, if you please!"

"You wot?" she said suspiciously. I simplified my request by pointing at the first draught pump I saw and made the sign of two with my fingers. This produced an even more hostile reaction, and the lady yelled over her shoulder "Frank, trouble." Within seconds a grey-faced, wiry little middle-aged man, surprisingly sprightly on his feet, appeared at our side clutching a baseball bat. "Woss goin' on Shirl?" he snarled, pacing about next to us.

Sensing a little hostility, I used the tactic I have always found the most effective: acting the ignorant tourist (this man didn't need to know that we had actually been residents of his little fiefdom for nearly a year now). "Ah, bonjour, monsieur le patron!" I said jovially. "We are les Francais on 'oliday. Your petit pub is tres charmant."

It was with some relief that we saw him break into a smile, revealing a set of interestingly stained, almost entirely pointed teeth. "It's just a couple of frogs, Shirl!" he said to his assistant. "Ere, bonjour and all that. What'll you be 'avin, then?"

The commotion had caused a small group of people to gather around us, and now that the tension had been diffused, the ambience turned into one of heartiness and good cheer. Old Shirley was kept busy on the pumps as the ale flowed and we got to know the regulars at the Catford Ram. They all bore similar characteristics: the sallow, leathery complexions of men who shun the outdoor life, eyes that seem to peer out from some musty cupboard of the soul, fingers silvered with the scratched-off panels of lottery cards. At first we presumed them to be participating in some traditional pub game or raffle, since they all clutched coloured scraps of paper bearing a number. But as we got to know them through the purchase of ales, we discovered they were all awaiting appointments with the Social Services, whose offices just around the corner were dedicated to the assistance of the jobless. Apparently the queues, organised by a system of numbered tickets, can be so lengthy that these wise gentlemen chose to wait their turn here in this cosy tavern, rather than among the hordes of migrant fraudsters they described as the principal visitors to the state benefit office.

Perhaps unintentionally, their descriptions made it all sound rather exciting. Our imaginations fuelled by seven or eight pints of lager by then, we pictured a scene straight out of 1st century Judea, with a cramped room full of hot-headed Abyssinians arguing over camel grazing rights and wailing Bedouins applying for Roman citizenry.

We settled up with the landlord, who presented us, now that our chums had returned to the dole office, with a bill for £179.73; we rememberred that there was still the shopping to do.

Tesco may be situated some twenty yards in a straight line from the Catford Ram, but it is a surprisingly difficult distance to manoeuvre at four o'clock in the afternoon when fuelled by eight pints of Stella Artois, a packet of Benson and Hedges and no lunch. Unfortunately I dropped one of the shopping bags from our earlier trip to the bargain stores, and an array of coloured plastic items went bouncing across the concrete into the entrance to Scope. Oh well, we reasoned, what comes around goes around.

According to the Gault-Millau, one will occasionally find in some of the British supermarkets a a counter assistant who really knows their stuff, perhaps a former local butcher or fishmonger forced out of business by his new employer. It was certainly something we were familiar with at home in Provence – the butcher who not only suggests certain cuts of meat for your proposed dish, but also gives you the correct herbs and explains how to cook it and what wine to drink with it.

"Which of your tasty viands would you recommend to make a delicious *pebronata*, young lady?" we asked the girl at the meat counter, charmingly attired in a traditional butcher's plastic apron and a faux straw hat. "You wot?" she replied.

I could see from her face that I was not speaking her language, and then it dawned on us that the purpose of our stay was to adapt to the local way of life. I abandoned my quest for *pebronata* ingredients, and asked her to furnish me with some ingredients for a typical local dish.

Veronique went in search of the pineapple rings that were to accompany our gammon steaks, while I went to peruse the wine section. As one of Aix-en-Provence's most respected vignerons, there was little that I did not know about wine. What immediately struck me about *le connoisseur Catfordois* was that, if Tesco's selection adequately reflected his needs, his palette tended towards the Teutonic. There was a large display of reduced bottles of Liebfraumilch surrounded by other simple Rieslings and something amusingly named 'Thunderbird Wine'. Our friends in the pub had informed us that, generally speaking, they only drink wine on special occasions, such as when they want to "get totally rat-arsed". We considered our credentials as *bons vivants* to be impeccable as the next man, but we drew the line at German wines.

Summer hath too short a lease, as the poet says, and so too has our sojourn in Catford. The vignerons of Provence beckon and it is time to turn our faces to France once more. As we pack our newly acquired velour leisure suits, souvenir underpants and a droll singing fish for old Marcel, Aix-en-Provence's finest Poissonier, memories flit back and forth like Costcutter bags in the number 54 bus shelter.

It truly has been an Annus Mirabilis. Our minds go back to the thrilling McDonalds riots of last summer, evening repasts at Dixy Fried Chicken, the eye-watering luminescence of the Catford Ram on a cold winter's eve and the spring festival of litter. We shall dearly miss our new friends. To the proud, reserved, stoical people of Catford: *salut à vous*! Here comes one now, old Alf, toiling up the stairs of Dregnor House with his familiar shopping chariot. I turn and raise my glass of WKD to him in valediction. "So, farewell Alf. I should like this opportunity to say…"

"Yeh. Bye."

"…or should I say '*au revoir*'?"

But Alf's door has slammed shut, and the sound of many bolts being drawn echoes down the concrete stairwell. There is nothing now but silence, with the odour of fried chicken and the almost-perceptible particles of pollution lingering in the air.

THE CHAP QUESTIONNAIRE

Nick Foulkes

Nick Foulkes is a sterling example of what is known in Fleet Street circles as a 'trouser journalist', penning articles for the broadsheet newspapers on all manner of gentlemanly accoutrements and activities. His erstwhile column in the *Evening Standard*, Ginger Fop, cast an appraising eye over sartorial pioneers of the past, and clearly came from a fellow who knew his Gieves & Hawkes from his Marks & Spencer. Mr Foulkes' biography of Count D'Orsay, *Last of the Dandies*, has just been published by Little, Brown.

What is your idea of complete sophistication?
Cary Grant in *To Catch A Thief*; Jean Pierre Martel at the wheel of his vintage Rolls Royce.

Who, in your opinion, is or was the quintessential English gentleman?
The Duke of Windsor in terms of dress; David Niven in terms of manner; Mark Birley in terms of suavity; Ian Fleming for his recognition of the importance of status-conferring goods.

And the quintessential lady?
My wife.

Name your three favourite items in your personal wardrobe.
This is an unfair question, and I find that with clothing as everything else, more really is more. I can however single out a double-breasted tweed suit with an alarming windowpane overcheck from Huntsman; a corduroy dinner jacket I had copied from one that I saw in the Duke of Windsor's wardrobe, and a pair of Russian calf slip-on shoes made for me by Eric Cook from 250-year-old reindeer hide tanned according to a process that was lost in the Russian Revolution.

What single situation has been the greatest challenge to your wardrobe and your personal grooming skills?
Recently I was nominated for (but did not win) the title Havana Man of the Year at the International Festival of Havana cigars in Cuba. I wore linen trousers, a teal blue single-breasted silk jacket from Huntsman, Budd voile shirt (double fronted), knitted silk Charvet tie in off-white (with an antique tie bar purchased at the Hotel Nacional that afternoon, for a little Meyer Lansky pre-Castro chic), blue checked Charvet pochette, Girard Perregaux wristwatch, and slip-on shoes from Pepe of

Marbella in blue and cream. I accessorized this with a limited edition cohiba cigar.

Which accessories would you never venture into polite society without?
Cigar cutter, Dupont lighter, Bentley motor car, full-size tournament backgammon set, small exquisitely bound volume of 19th century French verse, full set of bespoke Dunhill luggage, Smythson visiting cards, two sorts of dinner jacket.

What items of clothing do you consider to be the height of vulgarity?
The 'fleece'.

Which aspects of contemporary life do you think are most prohibitive of a gentlemanly lifestyle?
Most aspects of contemporary life militate against gentlemanly living – you try going to Ikea and asking to be directed to the day bed department.

How do you think young people can be prevented from becoming bad mannered, sportswear-clad ruffians?
Early visits to such destinations as Davidoff of London where young people can be inculcated into such arcana as cigar selection. Otherwise I would be quite happy to see association football prohibited and replaced by public broadcasts of backgammon tournaments, and compulsory classes on glove etiquette and top hat management to whatever level it is that equates to the old 'O' Levels.

What vices, if any, do you believe are conducive to beauty of mind and independence of spirit?
The reading of French poetry, frequent applications of Caron's Coup de Fouet or Creed's Tabarome, fine cigars.

Howard Spent investigates

THE SEMIOTICS OF LEGWEAR

If any part of a gentleman's body can be regarded as primitive, atavistic and primordial then surely that part is his leg. Often unattractively hirsute, a man's lower limbs have been designed by Mother Nature solely for the purposes of running from enraged mammoths or pursuing the raw ingredients for an evening repast.

Thankfully, due to the glories of the internal combustion engine and the growing trend for the home delivery of comestibles, the leg is now close to becoming totally redundant. Freed from the tyranny of hunting for his supper, the modern dandy is able to concentrate on what he does best: remaining motionless upon the chaise longue for days on end.

However, before the literalists among us resort to contacting a reputable surgeon for the removal of these offensive articles, it should be borne in mind that, even in this day and age, evolution has not progressed to such a point where the legs can happily be jettisoned altogether. There are still a few residual functions for which the legs must sadly be retained.

Legs can come in frightfully handy for transporting a fellow to and from the cocktail cabinet, literary salons and the opera etc, and it should not be overlooked that they also fulfil the important role of keeping the feet firmly attached to the body. After all, how else would one be able to display one's sterling collection of hand-crafted footwear?

In a few million years the wonders of natural selection will no doubt have found a solution to these tricky dilemmas, but in the meantime man has come up with some splendid stopgaps for the disguise and concealment of his sub-abdominal appendages. One of the greatest achievements of civilisation to date has been the invention of an elegant array of leg coverings, in pleasing patterns such as herringbone, Prince of Wales check and a multitude of tweeds, which have the effect of hiding the shameful bestiality of the

knees and giving a fellow's pins an elegance and hauteur they quite frankly don't deserve.

But beware, although there are many forms of legwear that lend dignity to the legs, there are far more that merely accentuate their anatomical absurdity and antediluvian origins.

Over the next few pages I have sought to convey a few brief observations, designed to enable the reader to distinguish between man-about-town and insufferable knave. I am sure you will find that they will prove an invaluable guide for use socially, in business, and for pleasure.

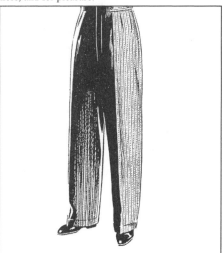

The Controlled

Although this fellow is possessed of the tempestuous and yearning soul of a poet, he utilises that zenith of civilised and pristine leg attire, the carefully creased Oxford bag, to keep his torrid imagination and animal sensuality strictly under check.

The Altruistic

This man's satin pantaloons and curly-toed slippers infuse his dinner guests with wistful visions of the exoticism of the Grand Tour. They are tremendously grateful, as it saves them from having to indulge in the beastly tedium of travelling abroad themselves.

The Sleazy

What sort of rudery is afoot here? This fellow regards himself as *a bit of a ladies' man,* but by displaying his nether regions in gaudy lycra like so many chitterlings on a butcher's slab he is more likely to send a lady into apoplexy rather than win her undying affection.

The Urban

Life is surely too short for indulging in desperately aspirational pastimes such as golf, but by donning plus fours and carrying a five iron on the city streets this fellow is amply equipped to repel the detrimental effects of dust, litter and criminally-inclined ruffians.

The Humorous

The outlandish antics of our celtic cousins are a great source of amusement for an Englishman. An inexplicable insistence on wearing plaid skirts in lieu of trousers, for example, makes a Scotsman an indispensable novelty that will enhance any wedding.

The Spiritual

Getting up of a morning and dancing to the sickly tune of Mammon is highly corrosive to one's appreciation of the Infinite. Any cove born with an instinct for the transcendent will spend at least 80% of his day in the comforting embrace of winceyette pyjamas.

The Vulgar

An unnatural regard for Miss Liza Minelli has once again caused the 15th Earl to scandalise the noble house of Camarden. If only he could be persuaded to use fish nets in the manly pursuit of angling rather than for a tawdry re-enactment of Weimar cabaret.

The Outrageous

Good God, this blighter seems to have mislaid the seat of his trousers. Sadly known as 'chaps', these immodest leg sleeves single this man out as a crazed homosexual. Watch out, fellow m'lad, such blatancy can only result in a criminal record or haemorrhoids.

The Slovenly

This man's torn denim trousers might lead one to pity the wearer as a unfortunate vagrant. Think again. He is actually a wealthy resident of Notting Hill who foolishly considers it somehow with-it and clever to dress like a common navvy. He deserves a good horsewhipping.

ALISTAIR CROOK'S
LETTER FROM T'NORTH

*Alistair Crook and his amusing chum Hankinshaw conduct an investigation
into the curious northern pastime of Bingo*

lthough it is widely accepted that the home of sophisticated, gentlemanly behaviour is to be found in the southern capital of this fair land, it may be of vague interest to wonder what the rest of Blighty gets up to whilst others are resplendent on the chaises longues of opium dens off the Embankment, or cavorting with unleaded prostitutes in the gin palaces of Whitechapel. To that end, I have been posted North by the editors of this slender publication in order to travel behind the looking glass of the M25 and report on what lifestyle options exist, in "t'North".

After being met at Covent Garden by said editors, I am immediately chloroformed and bundled aboard the mail train leaving from King's Cross, and, after two hours of Harry Houdiniesque wriggling around in a sack and straight jacket, tumble onto platform 5 in Northerntown.

Within a dozen minutes I am furnished with a travelling companion, a fellow called Miles Benedict F. Hankinshaw, whom I meet in Robin Hood/Little John fashion, brawling over the last bottle of absinthe in the booze aisle of Mr Netto's Grocerious Appallorium. (From various graffiti in bus shelters, I believe the 'F' in Hankinshaw's name to stand for 'Fiona' but I am loath to press this point.) Happily, he is a native of these parts, and

promises to furnish me with advice and kindly support. And so to the mission.

Naturally our first thought is entertainment. What does a fellow do in these parts for a little amusement? I am advised, by the kindly lady at the Post Office, that not only is Thursday night at the Bingo free, but that alcohol can be purchased at a reasonable price and, moreover, it has central heating – an equation of which any straight thinking gentleman would approve. Therefore I, and that maladjusted cove Hankinshaw, make our way out for an evening's fun.

On our arrival at what is popularly known as 'Mucca Bingo', we are immediately impressed by the extravagant carpet, which reminds one of those magic eye devices of the 1990s, where, if one stares too hard, a unicorn leaps out of the pattern and challenges one to a fight in the pub car park after hours. We are soon swept away from this downward gazing by the lady who will be our hostess for the evening, and, by the time we are asked to leave, will be calling herself our "Auntie" and threatening to smack the back of our legs. Her great excitement at our attendance forbids her from calling us by our correct names (she opts for Colin and Georgina), but she does tell us off when we become over-ambitious, clears up our accidental alcohol spillage and even leaves her dentures at our table. We suspect

that if we were to ask her nicely she would seek, amongst the bingo populace, a potential Mrs Hankinshaw for that frightful revolutionary with whom I have thrown in my lot. I wonder whether he would have the strength of mind to resist the offer of an ample-bosomed 60-year-old.

But "Auntie" is not the only person of interest. The caller is a fellow named Kingsley, and many people are keen to inform us that he has appeared on the popular children's television programme, *The Weakest Link*, presented by Roy Castle and Emu. As many readers will know from their childish seaside holidays, bingo calling mainly involves crying out, "clickety-click, forty-eight, two skinny swans, seventy-two, the major and his walking stick, one hundred and eleven"; but not this fellow. He dashes through the rules like a horse racing commentator: "nexgame-fullousecalloutforafullouseyellowpage… you're next, three and five, thirty-five".

Once Kingsley begins crying out numbers, the game is afoot. Being novices, and Auntie having vanished, we have little to do but stare around us and listen to the Sounds of "t'Bingo". After a holy silence descends, the crazy tribal jungle drum sound of "bingo dabbers" being repeatedly smashed against their cards begins, only to be interrupted by a native call of "line", "housey-housey" or "geeeeoooooooooor-rrrrrr", at which point the remainder of the players groan, and this is a groan that becomes more aggressive as the night goes on.

Of course, by this point, that louche oppressor Hankinshaw is overly excited and has begun screeching "Owzat!" at every given opportunity. He has also attempted to prove the high level of concentration present by dashing round the room wearing naught but his Marylebone sock garters (naturally I avert my eyes). People are beginning to stare at us, particularly the confident lady who is able to play bingo and do her knitting at the same time.

When two hours have flitted by like a snail dragging an anvil, our time has come and we flee without grace. As would you, dear reader, we sprint into the night; shrieking wildly like schoolgirls and waving our hands above our heads. We seek sanctuary in a quiet old men's pub where we move toward the light ale. That reckless degenerate Hankinshaw and I swear to each other that we shall never again be exposed to such vulgar, unsportsmanlike ruffians.

In the next issue, Alistair Crook and Hankinshaw tackle Association Football.

Howard Spent investigates

THE SEMIOTICS OF PETS

It has been observed within the confines of these pages before (but surely bears reiteration), that the desire to keep domestic pets is as unfathomably vague in the purpose as the propensity for otherwise rational human beings to spend vast amounts of their precious time in the rearing of children. Nevertheless, it is still an urge that millions of our fellow countrymen succumb to on a regular basis and should therefore not be overlooked by the trained semiologist merely because he finds it absurd or distasteful. The need to pamper and coset a mawkish array of creatures for their companionship, loyalty or aesthetic value persists and therefore any shrewd man of science should be prepared to bring his observant eye to the fore and glean what he can from the spectacle.

Even from the earliest age, Dear Reader, we learn to judge our peers by the pets they decide to keep. In the callow days of youth our judgements may be crude and unsophisticated, but who can say they were not secretly impressed when Wilkinson from Lower Sixth Beta turned up in the common room sporting a vicious rat or loquacious mynah bird on his shoulder. Or, alternatively, the sneering pity that one had for Plumpston Junior as he proudly exhibited the foolish looking chinchilla that his parents had bamboozled him into accepting as a viable Christmas gift item.

When a friend, neighbour or colleague reveals that he or she has recently purchased a new pet, or we observe someone walking down the public thoroughfare accompanied by some beast or other, we will naturally be lured into speculating what manner of man (or woman) would wish to be seen in such company.

On many occasions an owner will choose a pet that mimics their own appearance. A brutish publican, for example, lured by the narcissism of his own ugliness might select a bulldog as his companion.

Others will opt for a pet that they believe gives them social kudos. A wellington-clad inhabitant of Clapham might opt for a reassuringly dull labrador to enable them to fit seamlessly in with their neighbours. Or a self-satisfied media type slumming it in the bohemian quarter might decide on a Bald Backed Andalusian Sprungi, as a denoter of their unshakable belief in their own eccentricity.

Over the following pages we will merely scratch the surface of the insights that may be gleaned, but without doubt you will find them invaluable for use socially, in business, and for pleasure.

The Diabolical

Some would assume that a man who brandishes an unfeasibly large anaconda is trying to compensate for inadequacies in the trouser department, but this cheery Satanist rarely receives any complaints from the enthusiastic maidens that he ritualistically deflowers.

The Irritating

Humboldt's Woolly Monkey is a clingy little blighter, and as difficult to shake off as a cloyingly affectionate ladyfriend. A fellow who solicits such sickly dependency must surely be sadly lacking in self-esteem and suffering from desperate insecurity.

The Chichi

Whilst a trusty canine such as an Irish Wolfhound can lend a man an air of uncompromising masculinity, the 15th Earl of Camardenshire has once again missed an opportunity to embrace normality by buying a diminutive poodle and naming it Trixibell Fluffytum Sequins.

The Fashionable

Romanian orphans and Brazilian street urchins are this season's must-have accessory in the borough of Islington. Dinner guests will gape in wonderment as your newly imported ward climbs up the curtains or mugs your neighbours for their jewellery.

The Bland

Only an unimaginative fool could regard a hamster as an enthralling pet. Indeed the only way to render a rodent even vaguely entertaining is by obliging it to reside under challenging living conditions, such as a brief sojourn at the bottom of one's tropical fish tank.

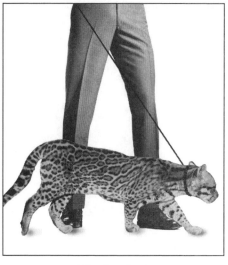

The Opulent

Much favoured by middle-aged homosexuals and mad old ladies, the cat is too cosy and predicable a pet choice to have much intrinsic style. By upgrading to an ocelot, however, one will win the respect of all and sundry when attending private views and premieres.

The Adolescent

Young hoodlums and spotty ne'er-do-wells often try to upset their parents by purchasing animals calculated to shock. Try interesting junior in an exotic bird such as budgerigar instead, but you should warn him that it is inadvisable to keep them in the same cage.

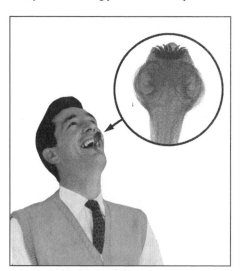

The Entertaining

Intestinal parasites are swiftly catching on as the only pet choice for those with a penchant for practical japes. Dormant for most of the day in its alimentary hideaway, a tape worm can be coaxed out, using morsels of canapé, to thrill the ladies at cocktail parties.

The Fanciful

Advances in genetic engineering have enabled the centaur to make a comeback as a viable pet option. Crossing the genes of one's manservant with those of a racehorse will not only result in decorative staff but also an outside chance in the 3.30 at Wincanton.

THE CHAP QUESTIONNAIRE

Richard Madeley

The deliciously inert will be familiar with the subject of our questionnaire, whose sprightly visage beams out from the television set as you tuck into tea, absinthe and crumpets after a lengthy afternoon snooze. Richard Madeley and his charming lady wife Judy provide a gentle hour of early evening persiflage on the fourth channel.

What is your idea of complete sophistication?

The silver engraving on my grandfather's Purdeys.

Who, in your opinion, is or was the quintessential English gentleman?

Leslie Howard. Come to think of it, the chap wasn't actually English. Colin Firth then, when the fellow remembers to wear a tie.

And the quintessential lady?

Greer Garson.

Where do you think the best-dressed people are?

Taking luncheon at Simpsons on the Strand.

Name your three favourite items in your personal wardrobe.

Cummerbund, father's gold cuff-links, and dress shoes from Church's.

Which aspects of contemporary life do you think are most prohibitive of a gentlemanly lifestyle?

General yobbishness on the streets; tobacconists' increasing over-familiarity; and the confounded cheek of London Underground staff who insist on referring to one as 'mate'.

What single situation has been the greatest challenge to your wardrobe and your personal grooming skills?

The day I was assaulted by a frightful chap I had the misfortune to interview – a bad hat, I'm afraid. I was rather tousled afterwards.

Which accessories would you never venture into polite society without?

Moleskin notebook, gold self-propelling pencil.

What items of clothing do you consider to be the height of vulgarity?

Socks in any colour other than black.

What vices, if any, do you believe are conducive to beauty of mind and independence of spirit?

The occasional top-quality shag in a briar.

Which view from which window would you describe as "a portal to sublimity"?

The view from my smoking-room window overlooking Hampstead Heath, where one often espies other chaps enjoying top-quality shags in the briars.

AnaChRoniSt

in THe
uK

Torquil Arbuthnot and Nathaniel Slipper outline the various methods by which a fellow may adopt the role of the gentleman anarchist.

One of the great disappointments of the demise of the last century and the infancy of this is how the younger, scruffy generation seems to be exerting their grubby influence on absolutely everything. Why, even our very own Prime Minister is often to be found drinking cups of tea, not from a bone China cup and saucer, but from a mug with the teaspoon still in it, not unlike the behaviour expected of a motor-lorry driver. One would hardly be surprised to hear that he had used the same mug to slurp an 'alcopopoholic' drink, or that his heart had to be maintained electronically. Even modern artists are no longer mightily bearded and bucolic gentlemen painting fine oils of Biblical scenes, or ladies whose clothes have given them the slip; but bumptious imbeciles who think nothing of sawing animals in half or publicly displaying the contents of their private bedchambers.

Likewise the demise of the noble anarchist, once huzzahed by the proletariat and feared by the ruling classes, working their mysterious ways, wearing their mysterious clothes, sidling to their mysterious meetings. Today's anarchist appears to be a well-to-do student, yet one who has foolishly chosen not to blow mama and papa's fortune on vintage port and single malt whisky, but on having mud and ordure smeared in their hair and rings placed in their noses, leading one to believe that their natural habitat should be the farmyard. Their devotion to anarchy involves standing outside American eateries shouting rowdily and disturbing the peace, before sneaking off to a different American eatery for a bucket of greasy batter masquerading as chicken, then retreating to the Halls of Residence to brag about how they so nearly brought down the government, usually to a response of utter apathy from their fellow students.

Happily, there is a far more glamorous, exciting and underworld side to the life of the gentleman anarchist, which can be yours by taking the following advice to heart.

The first person who will delight in your new persona will be your tailor. As you first enter his Jermyn Street premises, he will be slightly alarmed and not recognize you, due to the sudden appearance of your now wild white hair (anarchism, while immediately halting baldness, does accelerate the hair-whitening process). Once he has come to realise your identity, he will immediately clasp your hand and express his unbridled joy at the sartorial possibilities that your new occupation will allow him. Few people dress with such exquisite enthusiasm as the gentleman anarchist. Along with providing you with a jet black frock coat with gold lining, stovepipe hat and black velvet cloak for your everyday activities, you will also require the many disguises that allow you to pass through society unnoticed in your nefarious activities, such as archbishop, field marshal, Home Secretary, policeman and vampire. It is also time to purchase the swordstick that you have promised yourself since kindergarten and make a vow never to even attempt to give up smoking again.

The anarchist will, of course, require further accoutrements. He will need bombs, and these must be proper bombs, round and black with the word 'bomb' written on them in stark white letters, and a fuse made from a long, curly piece of hemp. Once the fuse is lit, one should comport oneself with courage and peace of mind, and carry the bomb in one's hand for at least a minute with no discernible increase in pace before releasing it only seconds before it explodes, bringing down an almighty amount of debris from the bourgeois abode at which it has been aimed, but leaving you, as always, utterly unruffled.

The Gentleman Anarchist will also be equipped with two revolvers (although blunderbusses are entirely acceptable). One of these is to be quite visible for the purpose of drawing attention to oneself during riots, or when surrounded by the mob, and a concealed one (preferably pearl-handled), which should only be revealed with considerable panache when one has apparently been disarmed and is about to be carted off to the Old Bailey and subsequently to Tyburn Tree. The use of a rifle may also be efficacious, for assassinations, whether of the religious or political variety, or even to dispatch an undercover policeman who may have infiltrated your company.

Thus, fully clad and armed, we now discover, and it is a relief to gentlemen such as ourselves, schooled in the art of idle frivolity, that the next stage of this dangerous lifestyle is complete inactivity. Of course, there must be great plans envisaged: the destruction of religion, the abolition and beheading of all members of the government and the constabulary, the liberation of colleagues from Parisian gaols, and the wanton guzzling of brandy. However, the gatherings where such extravagant undertakings are discussed are little more than the debating societies that you will remember from your days at Oxford. After a lengthy and meaningful squabble about the choice of a new password for the group, one's leader may go on to propose the question 'Qu'est-ce que c'est toute la propriété?' The predictable answer is that it is theft, but that is not to prevent any subsequent argument rumbling on into the night. If a frock coat is borrowed, for example, who is the thief, the wearer or the lendee? If the wearer has no intention of returning it, is it theft, but also property? Many hours are likely to pass before one of your number, probably one of the so-called self-styled intellectual working class will proclaim, 'Balls to this, I'm off for a spot of poaching', at which point the whole stimulating debate can begin again.

Moreover, whilst great plans can be formulated (deposing the Archbishop of York for example, and replacing him with an anarcho-syndicalist committee), who amongst the gathering can truly be trusted? The world of anarchism is sadly yet excitingly rife with undercover peelers. Who can tell if the wild-eyed gentleman on the left, who provided the group with hand grenades, is only interested in increasing his standing at Scotland Yard? Or if the callow-faced youth standing opposite has been trained since his Cambridge days to infiltrate and report back? The only people who can be trusted are those who can prove a link to the Russian aristocracy (this is, of course, true of absolutely anything in life).

Thus, a gentleman with time on his hands, a desire for dazzling attire and a terminal laziness could do worse than pledging himself to the anarchist movement. A dress code that even the Duchess of Whitby's daughter would find irresistible, a new circle of friends, acquaintances and enemies, and a need to achieve little except sit around a table in the dark shadows of a tavern squabbling is a perfect way to fill the idle months between the Oval test match and the Boat Race.

Suggested further reading

In Engels' Footsteps, T.P. Mariner
The Man Who Was Thursday, G.K. Chesterton
Five and the Black Hand Activists, Enid Blyton
1908 Baedeker Guide to St Petersburg

The
DECADENT  KITCHEN

Medlar Lucan

Our new gastronomic correspondent will provide The Chap with indispensable advice on roasting hedgehogs, stewing flamingoes and stuffing squid with calf brains. But first, a visit to a Viennese vinegar keller.

Since the police closed down our restaurant, The Decadent, in 1994, my co-author Durian Gray and I have lived a life of exile and adventure, wandering from place to place in a haze of squalor, excess and debt-spangled luxury. From time to time we retreat to a small cabaret-brothel in Old Havana, where we recharge our flagging accumulators in an atmosphere of hot, palm-fringed transvestism. Then we set off again, braving the ghastliness of international airports, to seek that ever-receding goal that hovers so tantalisingly beyond each horizon: the extravagant, the bizarre, the *new*.

In January this year, we were invited to Vienna, where the painter Paul Renner had announced the lunatic plan of forging a replica of the Decadent Restaurant at the Kunsthalle Museum. Despite our incredulity, he pressed ahead with the scheme, hiring waiters, chefs, set-painters, a mobile kitchen, the contents of a Masonic museum, as well as glasses, cutlery, china, tables and chairs from the Austro-Hungarian Imperial Furniture Depot. The result was outlandish yet oddly pleasing, a kind of Biedermeier Aztec décor, which, to our amazement, gave a remarkably accurate flavour of the original. Nothing, of course, could ever recapture the vanished effulgence of our temple of purple gastronomy, but this was a noble attempt. The Hell Fire Dining Club, as it was called, caused a sensation in Vienna.

One of its most striking details was a collection of glass flagons filled with amber, rose, violet and pumpkin-hued fluids. These had arrived on handcarts propelled by a pixie-like

figure with shining eyes and shoulder-length hair, sheathed in a suit of such exquisitely tailored, drainpipe-trousered elegance that all heads turned to look. The man in the suit was Erwin Gegenbauer. In the flagons was his life's obsession: vinegar.

I found my curiosity hard to contain. Not only was Herr Gegenbauer a notable dandy, but also that rare bird, a *novelty*. He invited me to visit his factory; I at once agreed; we made an appointment, and, one snowy afternoon about a week later, I found myself entering a drab grey building in the city's 10th district. I was led down a narrow, winding staircase to a cellar where, beneath a ceiling hung with spiders' webs, a small crowd had gathered. Herr Gegenbauer, in a charcoal and cream deerstalker and astrakhan reefer jacket, was holding forth. Here were some 40 different vinegars, flavoured not by the usual system of adding herbs or fruit to a standard vinegar but by a much purer and more laborious method: first creating a wine from the juice of each fruit, then turning the wine to vinegar by introducing a specific strain of bacteria. The result? He begged us to judge, splashing a few drops of each brew into the hollow beneath the tongue from a delicately poised pipette. This elaborate ceremony was not only picturesque, it also bypassed the lips (a hot-bed of gustatory prejudice, according to Herr G), allowing the flavour to be perceived directly by the tongue and nose. We tried raspberry, quince, melon, blackcurrant, fig… All soft, fresh and unmistakably redolent of the original fruit – at times, I fancied, of the Garden of Eden itself.

We moved to a zone of racks and oak bar-

rels, where sherries and sweet wines from late-harvested grapes are aged. In went the pipette. Out came a series of sweet-sharp nectars that hovered on the razor's edge between dessert wine and vinegar. One would willingly quaff such essences for breakfast. While my mind raced to further, non-culinary uses for these fluids – so delicately hermaphroditic! – we came to the next stage of the tour: a sampling of vinegar-washed cheeses. Glasses of red Zwiegelt wine and hunks of rustic bread could not disguise the incendiary nature of these palate-searing purgatives, which rapidly restored the balance between mind and body and savagely re-enthroned the lips as the arbiters of taste.

"I hope this is all decadent enough for you, Herr Lucan!" said our host.

"Nothing is ever *quite* decadent enough for me, Herr Gegenbauer," I replied. "It's a concept like the speed of light or Absolute Zero, a limit of the physical world beyond which things simply shatter or cease to exist. But if you were to ask me if such vinegars have a place in the Decadent Kitchen…"

I reflected that Herr G was a fine example of decadence himself. Ten years ago he inherited the family business, with a staff of 650 and a roaring trade in pickled beetroot and gherkins for the supermarkets of Eastern Europe. There was just one problem: he was bored stiff by his own products. So he switched to vinegar, shrank the business, and now has seven employees, producing a rare and exquisite commodity. Rather than chasing the masses, he invites them to come to him – having refined their palates and wiped their feet at the door. One can only wish Burger

King, Iceland and Wal-Mart would follow suit.

On taking my leave, I ask Herr Gegenbauer for some practical tips. Could he suggest a vinegar for the Working Man? 'Elderberry Balsamic', he says, with its muscular build and powerful, sweaty finish. And for the Gentleman? Undoubtedly a Muscatel Balsam: delicate, fragrant, aged for 10 years. And for a Lady? At the mention of the gentle sex, Herr G becomes thoroughly romantic – reflecting with a faraway look that selling vinegar to ladies is, for him, 'a profoundly erotic experience', which he likes to conclude with a bottle of Trockenbeerenauslese, made from the sweetest and lushest of dessert wines. And so a final question: is vinegar an aphrodisiac? In the right circumstances, he says, it can be. But it's also a potent restorative. Splash a little Apple Balsamic on a chapped member and, no matter how raw it may be, it will soon be back to its old bright, cheery appearance and ready for action. Now there's a tip for a gentleman!

Gegenbauer Vinegars can be bought at their shop in Vienna's open-air food market, the Naschmarkt, or online at www.gegenbauer.at

The Decadent Cookbook, by Medlar Lucan and Durian Gray, is published by Dedalus, as are *The Decadent Gardener* and *The Decadent Traveller.*

Professor Pinkerton's
REPORT FROM THE
SMOKING ROOM

PIPES, PLEASURE AND THE SMOKING CLASSES

Pipe smoking has recently cropped up on *The Chap*'s letters pages, chiefly in warnings about potential lavatorial disasters, so it seems timely to provide all you puffing billies out there with some information and observations on the world of nicotinian delight, as experienced through man's best friend, his trusty briar.

A sure sign of a fellow Chap, in street, bar or betting-office, is that unmistakable wooden protuberance held jauntily in his chops. Indeed, evidence of a highly experienced Chap may be observed in the co-ordinated angles of his pipe and headgear. To the non-cognoscenti, the employment of this strange contraption, belching filthy smoke and spattering ashes at regular intervals, and with its potential health hazards, may seem like a curious left-over from some ritual buried deep in human prehistory. But in fact this is not so, for although our ancestors smoked herbal concoctions for medicinal purposes thousands of years ago, the spread of the seductively intoxicating *Nicotiana tabacum*, from its homelands in the Americas (whose populations had long venerated its benefits),

is a relatively recent phenomenon, a by-product of the age of "discovery" in which European conquerors, adventurers, settlers and traders of the 16th and 17th centuries started what we might now call the globalization of culture (those whom they "discovered" would probably describe the process less favourably).

Renaissance Chap (skilled in all civilised mores and in all branches of *scientia*, but nevertheless challenged in matters of tweed and trilby) would not have smoked the familiar briar. The early pipe-smoking era was dominated by clay pipes, porcelain pipes, the *calabash* (from a gourd), the famous water pipe (or hookah) and the carved *Meerschaum*, ('foam of the sea' in German), made from highly compressed deposits of sea shells on the bed of the ocean, dating back some 50 million years, raised millions of years later by geological action to within a few hundred feet below the earth's surface. It can be carved into a variety of fanciful shapes and is gradually stained a rich brown by the tobacco oils.

But for everyday use, a Chap's oral incendiary habits will be dominated by the briar pipe, whose development in the later 19th

century transformed the enjoyment of nicotian pipiculture. The name comes from the French *bruyere*, for a Mediterranean tree on whose roots grows a "burl" of very strong and heat-resistant wood. Bowl shapes and sizes are legion, often with manufacturer's own styles, but the main types are widespread and have names more or less reminiscent of their profiles (such as billiard, apple, pot, brandy, horn), their image (such as bulldog and diplomat) or some national association (such as Dublin, Dutch or Rhodesian). Bowls may have polished or blasted surfaces, and their stems (normally vulcanite) may be straight or bent. It always seems to amuse other customers when one requests a Bent Rhodesian in the tobacconist's shop.

There is a refreshing quantity of accompanying paraphernalia: chenille pipe cleaners, reamers to cut back the carbon accumulation in the bowl, knives to cut tobacco, tampers to pat the burning cake, spikes for a clogged bowl, matches, lighters, and jars, tins and pouches for the precious tobacco itself.

And what of the tobacco – the holy leaf whose worship lies at the heart of this great social ritual, whose nicotine provides both its essential character and its potentially addictive quality? It too, like the briar bowl for which it is destined, is the product of painstaking preparation – from harvesting, through maturing, drying, and grading through to its final appearance as the plug, flake or loose mixture over whose purchase the pipe-smoker lovingly lingers. Particular characters can be derived from distinctive tobaccos or preparations, such as Turkish Latakia, the Dutch scented aromatics and the American-inspired fruit and drink flavoured tradition which is now very popular.

As a pipe-smoking Chap you are a member of a wonderful fraternity. Pull out your pipe

in public and you are bound to be approached by at least one fellow journeyman and engaged in some question of tobacco blending or briar shape. A heavy pocketful of paraphernalia and ash stains down one's clothes are small prices to pay for the hours of pleasure involved in keeping your pipe alight for the occasional few minutes. Be faithful to your briar, but play the field from time to time – if you are bored with your usual Bent Bulldog, you can always try an exotic hookah. And finally, remember to buy good quality accessories, for they will last you to the grave.

THE TEN STEPS TO PIPULAR NIRVANA

1. Break in a new pipe by slow-smoking, indoors, carbonising the bowl using a few half-fills.
2. Maintain the carbon cake, to protect the bowl from burning, by cutting back with a reamer.
3. Fill the bowl by trickling the tobacco, then tamp down, repeating until the bowl is almost full; draw on the pipe to test that it is clear.
4. Employ two-stage lighting – first to char the whole surface, second to ignite it.
5. Achieve an even burn by regular and slow drawing on the mouthpiece.
6. At intervals shake off loose ash, tamp the surface flat with the tamper and re-light.
7. Avoid spittle flowing down the pipe-stem by keeping your tongue off the mouthpiece.
8. Empty the bowl of dottle (debris) when finished using the reamer (do not bang against hard surface).
9. Leave a pipe cleaner in the stem after smoking, with the bowl placed lower than the mouthpiece (i.e. on a pipe rack).
10. If smoking at least once every day, keep several pipes to ensure proper drying.

THE CHAP QUESTIONNAIRE

Edward Tudor Pole

The subject of our questionnaire is a songwriter and musician best known for his beat group of the late 1970s, Ten Pole Tudor. Also an actor, he is soon to appear as Spike Milligan in the forthcoming moving picture *The Life and Death of Peter Sellers*. Mr Tudor Pole describes his latest one-man show featuring words and music as "unsuitable for anyone over 29". *The Chap*, therefore, apologises for being unable to supply any further information.

What is your idea of complete sophistication?
Eating paté off the firm flat belly of a young beauty without giving any thought as to how sophisticated one is, or isn't.

Who, in your opinion, is or was the quintessential English gentleman?
Is Edward Fox, was Gerald du Maurier.

And the quintessential lady?
My maternal grandmother, née Cecilia Streeten. "Never brown in town," she said.

Where do you think the best-dressed people are?
The best dressed are likely to reject the filth of the city as an environment for their proper attire, where everyone appears to favour artificial fibred casual-wear, and elect to live in the countryside.

Name three favourite items in your personal wardrobe.
A pair of black brogues bought from a tramp 20 years ago and still going strong. A houndstooth suit tailored by Mark Powell, and an American southern states bull's head string tie; not entirely gentlemanly for an Englishman perhaps, but then neither am I.

What single situation has been the greatest challenge to your wardrobe and your personal grooming skills?
Deciding what to wear when I had to give a lecture on punk rock. After much thought I opted for formal dinner dress. The right decision.

Which accessories would you never venture into polite society without?
A handkerchief, a cigarette lighter and polished shoes.

What items of clothing do you consider to be the height of vulgarity?
'Trainers' worn when not playing sport, but most heinous of all, when worn with a suit.

Which aspects of contemporary life do you think are most prohibitive of a gentlemanly lifestyle?
Socialists. It may seem a good idea to militate for an equal society, but what actually happens is that everything becomes equally mediocre and second rate. To lead a gentlemanly lifestyle is seen by such misguided people to be elitist. I would like a society in which everyone was equally gentlemanly.

How can young people be prevented from becoming bad-mannered, sportswear-clad ruffians?
Good manners should specifically be taught at state schools by gentle people for two hours a week, with lavish praise and prizes awarded for attainment and progress made. Organised sport should be compulsory for young people at least twice a week, then they would learn what sportswear is for. Demolish tower blocks and create playing fields. They would welcome this.

Which view from which window would you describe as "a portal to sublimity"?
The view of the entrées following the paté.

CHARIOTS
OF COCOA

It has been four uneventful years since men lacking in substance dusted down their flannels, polished their rosewood briars and embarked on a rigid training schedule under a table in the Lamb & Flag. But, as Torquil Arbuthnot and Nathaniel Slipper report, the 17th Chap Olympics look set to put Regent's Park back on the A-Z

"**B**ring me your tired, your poor, your sick, and make them run around and jump up and down," goes the Olympic motto; and once again the four-yearly cycle has turned and it is time for the great athletic event. However, a true gentleman, rather than being forced to sprint around some Greek building sites in tight clothing, sweating and getting muddy knees, will make his way gently to Regent's Park, home of the 17th Chap Olympiad. This we are delighted to take part in, for, despite the use of false passports, moustaches and aeroplanes, we have been unable to sneak through customs of the Hellenic paradise where we ouzoed away much of our lamentable youth.

Once again, it is with great pride that dear old Blighty is asked to host this momentous event, and the only request that one puts to Lord Olympic is that, in return, no competitive Americans are allowed to enter.

The Olympiad itself is akin to the beloved sports days of our youth, even down to the be-flannelled teachers wandering around the greensward with clipboards, desperately trying to finish things off before sloping to the Wagon and Horses. In appropriate fashion, the Chap Olympics are not about winning, but trying to avoid taking part. Happily most of the events take up very little effort, and, to the dilettante gentleman, training is akin to cheating.

Usually at the counting up of the baubles and medals at the end of the afternoon, it is a clean sweep for Britain. It has to be noted that all the events take place in only one competition, and are then entirely replaced for the next competition. This is to prevent our Australian cousins from spending the next four years and their entire scientifical budget on practising and becoming good at any of these fine sports. As a people, they show an inappropriate level of competitiveness that is not becoming on this chivalrous occasion.

The games open with the lighting of the Olympic pipe, which is filled with an agreeable mixture of Greek Shag and Captain Cavendish's Premium Aromatic. The pipe is then ceremoniously paraded around London Zoo by a variety of gentlemen, pausing only to buy an ice-cream cornet. And then the mighty contest begins.

The opening event is the relating of anecdotes, the traditional opening line of which is: "I say, that reminds me, gentlemen, of a rather amusing story I should like to impart." The judges keep a keen eye on the quality of the punchline, the amount of guffaws received during the telling of the tale, and the ability to end the same story that was begun, rather than changing anecdotes several times.

This is followed by the 10-yard saunter. Fellows still huddle in corners and talk about the proud moment when Sir Nicholas Seabeggar broke the fourteen-minute barrier for this event. At the time it was feared that Sir Nicholas might explode or his skin fall off, but the world record he set in 1932 has yet to be beaten.

Throwing the quill is the next exciting event, which sees fiery-haired poets gently bowl their quills onto the park, with cries of "Alack, alas, woe is me, I am rent asunder," and other such melancholy mouthings. Next, the royal party, where dukes and barons take part in the Fabergé egg and spoon contest, in which they amble round showing off their wealth and looking intolerably smug. This soon ends, when the judges make great play of having to inspect these expensive gewgaws before scarpering with them. Inevitably they turn out to be cheap forgeries, and one of the morals of these games is that the landed gentry are not to be trusted.

The apathy marathon is one of the definitive events of the Chap Olympics. This begins with gentlemen examining their pocket watches and murmuring to each other that the pubs have now opened. Once ensconced in a snug with pints of foaming ale, a careful analysis of the games still to be played takes place. This can last for at least an hour longer than the remaining events would have taken. Eventually, to much nodding of the head, the rest of the Chap Olympics are cancelled and the party move on to the Lamb and Flag for all round celebrations.

And so for another quadrennium, the athletic event of the season retreats to an elderly man's briefcase, to gather dust in his attic until 2008. Another glorious triumph and many golden medals for plucky Britain and a yah boo sucks to anybody who believes in training and going without fine red wine and Turkish gaspers. Meanwhile, in the pub, the committee, comprising of all those still vaguely upright, begins squabbling over which events will take place in the next competition. This can last for several days and will be utterly forgotten within fifteen seconds of the end of the conversation.

OTHER EVENTS IN THE 2004 CHAP OLYMPICS

Hat doffing (the most number of different doffs within a timed minute).

Who can shout loudest at a foreigner and still come away without having bought stamps/tobacco/a glass of Madeira.

Shooting the cuffs.

Making a glass of brandy and cigar last for as long as possible while the competitors sit in armchairs discussing politics and economics.

The Raffles Event, where the Chap has five minutes in which to shin up a drainpipe in full evening dress, clamber through a sash-window and empty a dowager's jewellery box.

Fisticuffs with ruffians who snigger at one's attire. The ruffians' arms are bound to their bodies for their own personal safety.

100-yard crawl through bushes, whilst evading one's creditors and/or a prospective father-in-law bearing a shotgun.

Discus (involving a plate of cucumber sandwiches to be wafted through the air without spilling a single sandwich).

Dressage event – accompanying a lady into Simpson's department store (competitors will be penalised for foot-faults, errors in deportment and sheer caddishness).

The Gentleman's Excuse-Me: an opportunity for the Chap competitor to 'scratch his name from the racecard' at the last moment, upon realising one has a prior engagement with one's tailor/turf accountant/mistress.

The training ground for events such as the 10-yard saunter. Note the particularly difficult home stretch, after consuming 17 straight single malts in the leather armchair on the right.

Training for the Chap Olympics can be excessively demanding, which is why there is very little of it. But, as Nathaniel Slipper found out when he was shown around the Chap Olympiad training centre in a room above the Lamb & Flag, contestants do not enter the competition entirely unprepared.

Athletes often require initial assistance with unfamiliar positions such as standing up

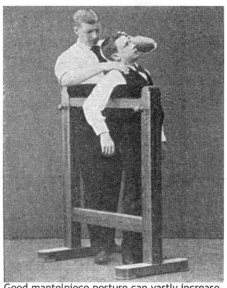

Good mantelpiece posture can vastly increase one's chances in the Relating of Anecdotes

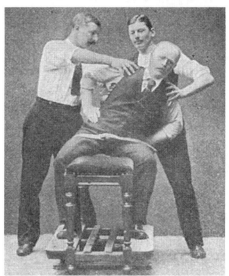

Trainers put an athlete through his paces for the gruelling cigar and brandy event

An athlete is prised off the apparatus after rigorous training for the 24-hour snooze event

CHAPPIST DISPATCHES

The Chap keeps a beady eye on gentlemanly activity around the globe. In this issue, **Tyrone Featherstonehaugh** reports on an incidence of disobedient civility by a brace of tweed-clad protesters, who took umbrage at some clumsy curating by London's Victoria and Albert Museum

25th May 2004, London Town... Seventeen followers of *The Chap* handcuffed themselves around Rachel Whiteread's 'Untitled (Room 101)' in the Cast Courts of the Victoria and Albert Museum. The Chaps and Chapettes formed a "human cufflink" around the 18x12-foot sculpture and recited the final lines of John Keats' *Ode on a Grecian Urn*: "Beauty is truth, truth beauty, – that is all/Ye know on earth, and all ye need to know."

The human cufflink produced no reaction whatsoever from security officers at the V&A, so the Chaps climbed on to the sculpture and continued the protest from its surprisingly wobbly surface. Even then, they were able to dispatch the contents of several hip flasks before attracting any attention.

A stand-off ensued between the tweed-clad protesters, emboldened by their unassailable height and whisky, and security guards. The Chaps' spokesman agreed with a negotiator for the V&A to come down, if provided with a stepladder and an ashtray.

The latter, alas, was not forthcoming, and the Chaps descended, one by one, with unsmoked pipes and cigarettes clasped between their teeth. Various members of curating and conservation staff then appeared and attempted to herd the Chaps into a corner to give them a good ticking off, having sealed off the exit from the Cast Court. There was only one course of action. The Chaps politely but firmly asked to be released, and, showing remarkable dignity, filed out of the V&A with a security escort.

For over a century, the Victoria and Albert Museum's Cast Court has been a repository of plaster reproductions of the world's great monuments, including life-size replicas of Trajan's column, the Pórtico de la Gloria in Santiago de Compostela and Michelangelo's David. Originally intended as a reference for classics and arts students unable to afford the Grand Tour, the Cast Court provided a place to contemplate some of the wonders of the cultural world.

Until, that is, November 2003, when public art consultants Modus Operandi invited Rachel Whiteread to install a piece of her work in the Cast Courts, because "the resonance and mythology of the space might fascinate her".

It seems, however, that the resonance and mythology of the space didn't fascinate Ms Whiteread, because she decided to make yet another plaster cast of an empty room, this time Room 101 at the old BBC Building, which George Orwell purportedly used as a reference for his Room 101 in the novel *1984*. But hold on a minute – what has this got to do with Trajan's Column?

"Room 101," says Ms Whiteread, "stands as a metaphor in the collective memory and the popular imagination for the worst thing that can happen to you." Indubitably, but where does Michelangelo's David fit in?

Not at all, is sadly the answer, since many of the plaster reproductions had to be moved out of the way to squeeze in Ms Whiteread's gargantuan cube of plaster. Studying the informative placard displayed next to the sculpture, one reads that, in fact, "Other casts in the gallery have been *arranged* by Rachel Whiteread". The result is that, from every angle, one's view of the other exhibits in Cast Court 46B are obscured by 'Untitled (Room 101)'.

By giving a single artist the exclusive privilege of reflecting on the contents of the Cast Courts, the V&A has denied the same pleasure to the general public. Visitors to Tate Modern, for example, are not forced to peer around classical sculptures in order to view someone shouting on a giant video screen. This clumsy bit of curating seems to reflect the fear held by all public museums of being perceived as stuffy and old fashioned. *The Chap* says: it's alright to be stuffy and old fashioned, and better than trying to keep up with the trendy crowd and getting it hopelessly wrong in the process.

FURTHER READING

If you enjoyed reading this book, why not subscribe to **The Chap** Magazine? This exquisite quarterly publication continues to offer advice on personal grooming, sartorial elegance and common courtesy. With a continually growing circulation and plaudits from Stephen Fry, John Cooper Clarke and Ian Hislop, **The Chap** has established itself as essential reading matter for those in search of their inner gentleman, their inner lady or simply a purveyor of quality brilliantine.

I would like to take out an annual subscription to **The Chap**.
I enclose a cheque made out to **The Chap** for £10.00.
My name and address are:

Name: ....

Address: ....

....

....

....

Please send a copy of this form to:
The Chap, PO Box 39216, London SE3 0XS
Subscribe online at **www.thechapmagazine.com**